HUMAN SERVICES

New Careers and Roles
in the Helping Professions

HUMAN SERVICES
New Careers and Roles
in the Helping Professions

By

ROBERT J. WICKS, Psy.D.

The Graduate School of Social Work and Social Research
Bryn Mawr College
Bryn Mawr, Pennsylvania

CHARLES C THOMAS · PUBLISHER
Springfield · Illinois · U.S.A.

Published and Distributed Throughout the World by
CHARLES C THOMAS • PUBLISHER
BANNERSTONE HOUSE
301-327 East Lawrence Avenue, Springfield, Illinois, U.S.A.

© *1978, by* CHARLES C THOMAS • PUBLISHER
ISBN 0-398-03777-9
Library of Congress Catalog Card Number: 77-27986

With THOMAS BOOKS *careful attention is given to all details of
manufacturing and design. It is the Publisher's desire to present
books that are satisfactory as to their physical qualities and artistic
possibilities and appropriate for their particular use.* THOMAS
BOOKS *will be true to those laws of quality that assure a good
name and good will.*

Printed in the United States of America
N-11

Library of Congress Cataloging in Publication Data

Wicks, Robert J
    Human services.

    Bibliography: p. 222
    Includes index.
    1 Social service—Vocational guidance. 2. Paraprofessionals in social
service—Vocational guidance. 3. Mental health services—Vocational
guidance. I. Title.
HV10.5.W5   361.0023   77-27986
ISBN 0-398-03777-9

For
Dorothy and Jack Barry

PREFACE

MODERN human services technology embraces the community mental health and new careers movements of the 1960s. Today, it touches practically everyone in some way, yet there is still much confusion in the minds of many regarding its antecedents, current status, and future potential.

Accordingly, this book was written in response to the questions that beginning students, new careerists, and novice professionals are now asking about human services in the United States. It was developed with the hope that it could provide one with a "flavor" of the movement's history and current direction.

The book is brief by design. A truly in-depth book—citing numerous studies—was considered inappropriate for the audience for whom it is intended i.e. students and practitioners desirous of a quick but complete overview of the area. *Human Services* is set up to serve as the primary text for a one-semester, undergraduate level course, or as a readable primer for professionals not completely familiar with the topic. For a more detailed treatment of any of the topics covered, a quite extensive bibliography is supplied at the end of the book.

Traditional mental health approaches and advances are discussed in the first part of the book. Since community mental health is very much a part of today's mental health scene, previous legislative and therapeutic milestones in this area are given special attention.

Part II presents an overview of modern mental health technology. It looks at the new careers movement, current treatment approaches, such as crisis intervention, and the roles played by new professionals and volunteers in mental health.

Part III of this volume represents the bulk of the book; it deals with a coverage of new roles and careers in the helping professions allied to psychology and psychiatry. These chapters include the police, courts, corrections, education, social work, and medicine. In each case attention is given to the recruitment, selection, training, and utilization of new professionals in the fields in question.

The final chapter is devoted to a presentation of some implications for the future of the human services. As one might expect, more questions are raised than can be answered.

Whether the readers are community college human services majors, or professionals in the behavioral sciences who thus far are not completely familiar with the bulk of the material contained in this text, the author hopes they walk away from this volume with an appreciation for the movement's complexity and inspirational creativity. While many of the concepts surrounding community mental health and the new careers movement are now coming into question, one point seems evident: Today's stage of development in the human services is a most necessary link between the limited services offered in the past and the needed additional progress required to meet the mental health needs of the future.

R.J.W.

ACKNOWLEDGMENTS

THIS BOOK attempted to draw information from many sectors in the human services. In this pursuit, the author called upon numerous persons and agencies for assistance. All of them will not be listed here, but this is not done from lack of gratitude, but for a lack of space.

With the above proviso, I would like to extend my thanks to Loretta Marsella of the Volunteer Action Council; Lt. C.T. Palamara, Miami Police Department; Don Fisher, National Institute of Mental Health; Hugh Rosen, Hahnemann Medical College; William Denham, NIMH; Alcoholics Anonymous; Recovery, Inc.; and the Mental Health Association of Southeastern Pennsylvania.

Naturally, I would also like to express my gratitude to the Mental Health Sciences Department of Hahnemann Medical College, along with Dr. Israel Zwerling, Chairperson, and Dr. Clifford DeCato, the Acting Director of Graduate Education in Psychology, who together have set the tone and provided the motivation to search and work in the human services.

Finally, I would like to thank my wife Michaele for her patience and support. Without her understanding and soft spoken encouragement, the final draft of the manuscript would never have been completed.

R.J.W.

CONTENTS

HUMAN SERVICES

New Careers and Roles
in the Helping Professions

PART I

TRADITIONAL MENTAL HEALTH WORK: FORERUNNERS OF MODERN HUMAN SERVICES TECHNOLOGY

Chapter 1

TRADITIONAL METHODS, SYSTEMS, AND STAGES IN MENTAL HEALTH TREATMENT

A REVOLUTION against the status quo in mental health is in the spotlight. All through the 1960s and into the 1970s there has been a great deal of talk about the necessity of using paraprofessionals, creating new careers, and establishing community mental health settings that can provide comprehensive and continuous care.

But what preceded this so-called revolution in the human services? If we accept that the current movement represents a fourth revolution, what of the other three?

In reflecting on these questions it becomes evident that to appreciate where we are now, two things should be done first: (1) the past, so-called traditional methods and advances in mental health should be viewed, and (2) the existing structure of mental health care just prior to the community mental health movement's major thrust should be examined. By looking at the way it was before, one can more easily see the source of resistance to innovation, since self-interest groups and rigid theorists can be expected to stand up for the status quo.

BRIEF HISTORY

Moral Treatment: First Revolution in Mental Health

Just as the current revolution might not seem important without being put into perspective, the "moral period," too, would not seem very earthshattering if a bit of the history before it were not briefly noted.

Though early healers and philosophers, such as Hippocrates, Aretaeus, Asclepiades, Galen, and Plato, did show an appreciation for what mental illness was that seemed quite modern in relation to the views held by some of their contemporaries, the

5

treatment for mental illness was primitive up to and during the moral revolution of the late eighteenth century. For instance, though forms of trephining (drilling holes in the head) and exorcisms were used as far back as the stone age, their practice is evident until modern times.

In medieval times, exorcism was an extremely common method of dealing with possession by the devil, which is generally held to have resulted in many forms of what we would now term as just eccentric and psychotic behaviors.

The types of treatment in asylums and institutions included the crib, a form of confinement, chains, and iron collars. The sick person was not helped; instead, he was restrained and often punished.

According to Deutsch (1946),

> The mentally ill were hanged, imprisoned, tortured, and otherwise persecuted as agents of Satan. Regarded as sub-human beings, they were chained in specially devised kennels and cages like wild beasts, and thrown into prison, bridewells and jails like criminals. They were incarcerated in workhouse dungeons or made to slave as able-bodied paupers, unclassified from the rest. They were left to wander about stark naked, driven from place to place like mad dogs, subjected to whippings as vagrants and rogues. (P. 53)

Pinel (1745–1826) came upon conditions as they were described above shortly after the French Revolution. With his appointment as director of La Bicetre in 1792, the moral revolution in mental health more or less officially began, the reason being that he—for the first time—began unshackling the chains of the mentally ill with the wary sanction of the local government. Instead of beatings, he was to try kindness and fresh air. It was a simple beginning, but one that was a radical departure from the sordid past.

Pinel also took a step toward instituting patients rehabilitation. He established structured activities for the patients, something almost unheard of at the time.

The first revolution was also spearheaded by Benjamin Rush, the "Father of American Psychiatry," and William Tuke, who developed a *Retreat* for patients. In this institution Tuke treated the patients as friends and guests. This Retreat served as a model for future ones that were established in America by his son Samuel.

Freudian Psychology: Second Revolution in Mental Health

Moral treatment had been primarily concerned with setting up environments which would permit alleviation of pain and an opportunity for re-education. Essentially, it was directed at the current patient population of the time as a group, more concerned in *doing* good for the greatest number than in developing theories of psychopathology and psychotherapy.

The second revolution was in sharp contrast to this emphasis. Sigmund Freud was a scientist and a great thinker. He was concerned with providing a scientific explanation of pathology more than anything else; treatment was important, but it was secondary to research for him. He was to be a giant among theorists in the area of psychopathology and psychoanalysis (a deep form of therapy designed to affect personality change) .

Freud's positive effect on the mental health movement was just as astounding as was his negative impact on the future *community* mental health approaches to treatment. While he was to be an impetus for great psychological and psychiatric thinkers, his focus on the individual and his belief in treating mental illness as a physical disease entity (medical model) was to forestall a community approach, which for many years considered the greatest good for the greatest number. While he redirected the cause of mental problems as coming from within the personality (intrapsychic) , attention was diverted away from interpersonal and societal factors which affect the incidence and form of mental illness.

Psychotropic Drugs: Third Revolution in Mental Health

When pressed on the inhumane treatment of patients in state institutions, the directors would pointedly reply that the constraints they used and the various shock therapies they employed were simply to protect the patients from hurting themselves and others. The same argument was used to support decisions not to release patients from an institutional environment. "Suppose they become violent?" "Surely you can see that he is acting very strangely; how do you expect him to function in the free community?"

In 1952, with the introduction of chlorpromazine (Thorazine®) and resperine to treat very unusual, abnormal (psychotic) behavior, these arguments began to fall by the wayside. No longer was physical force necessary. Now chemicals could be used to control, to clear up thoughts that were bizarre, and to relieve some of the agitation.

The initial result of the discovery of drugs that worked with the mentally disturbed was to use their effects to replace large staffs. Drugs were used to "snow" patients. In other words, instead of the patients being controlled by mechanical devices, they were given large doses of drugs so they would become dizzy if they moved too quickly and ultimately stuperous if kept at that drug level.

The secondary impact of the discovery of psychopharmacological agents (also referred to as psychoactive/psychotropic drugs) was to be quite beneficial to patients and was a major thrust for the establishment of mental health centers in the community. When it was found out, for example, that daily dosages of certain antipsychotic drugs, i.e. ones used with the very bizarre or disturbed individual, could aid in decreasing hyperactivity, eliminating destructive behavior and hallucinations (sensing things without physical cause for them) and improving interpersonal and hygienic activities, there was a move to release institutionalized patients into the community more quickly.

The feeling was being accepted by those currently in or on the threshold of authority in psychology, psychiatry, and social work that people no longer had to be isolated from the community. With drug therapy, the patient could now be kept with or quickly returned to the neighborhood and family from which he had come. This was very important, for studies had long shown that state institutions had proven useless and oft times harmful to the patients they were supposed to be treating. Thus the stage was set for the community mental health movement.

Community Mental Health: Fourth Revolution in Mental Health

Presently we are in the midst of the fourth revolution, the era of the community mental health center. The basic underlying premise of this immediate stage is to provide comprehensive and continuous care for people where they live and work. In essence, the theory is based on the belief that it is best to treat them where they are.

Up to this point the trend was to hospitalize and institutionalize. Now, even in the case of chronic schizophrenics who have been seriously disturbed for years, the hope is that, with sophisticated outpatient care, this group can be kept in the community.

Among other things, these community mental health centers were to provide emergency, in-patient, out-patient, partial hospitalization, and consultant services. They were to be decentralized so that they would be available to serve people in their own communities. Each center would have satellite clinics and teams so that a person would not have to go far for help.

The team would be interdisciplinary. There would be various professional workers, and a new expanded cadre of new careerists (an untrained resident of a poverty area who seeks a position at entry level which would provide the needed education to advance to full professional status), such as a mental health worker, community health aide, or human services worker, to provide assistance. Outreach workers chosen from the communities themselves would go back to their neighborhoods and make the people aware of the services available in *their* local centers for mental health (Panzetta 1971; Whittington 1972; Beigel and Levenson 1972).

TRADITIONAL TREATMENT MODALITIES

Up to and including the most recent movement in mental health treatment, there were a number of treatment approaches in widespread use. They include psychotherapy, drug therapy, surgical procedures, convulsive therapies, and occupational therapy.

These modalities were administered by a carefully segregated team of licensed professionals, assisted by unappreciated, ill-trained assistants or attendants, through an organized system that often discriminated against the financially less fortunate. The premise for treatment was that the patient was in the need of help from a professional—preferably an M.D., but a Ph.D. psychologist or a M.S.W. (master's degree person in social work) were often deemed acceptable *under the supervision of a physician.*

The private office and clinic, as well as the stylish "rest center," were designated for the wealthy, with the state and general hospitals for the less well-off. The nurse, psychiatric aide, and occupational-recreational assistants were all in the background. Their training in psychopathology and treatment was either nonexistent or based on the medical model. Thus, though they saw the system was unequal and not working for the most part, they were not in a position to have great impact—even though it was they, not the doctors of psychology and psychiatry, who spent a great deal of time in direct contact with the patient population.

Elitism

Just prior to and during the fourth revolution of mental health, not only were the traditional methods of approach in obvious evidence, but the organizations and associations of the traditional professional helpers fought to keep the status quo. The psychiatrists—despite the voices of Szasz, Maxwell Jones, and Laing—fought to maintain their supremacy over both professionals, i.e. psychologists, and new professionals. The psychologists warned about permitting untrained mental health workers to do sophisticated diagnostic work. And the social workers' key association was almost cut in two by the debate over admission of social service personnel who possessed only a bachelor's degree.

The scene on which the community mental health movement was to arrive was not a conducive one for healthy development. Instead, there was much dissention over whether traditional modalities of treatment could or should be utilized in the community mental health setting, and if so, who should be empowered to administer them to the public. Instead of the existing associations assisting in the development of new careers and treatment techniques, they often stymied efforts at progress whenever they saw such advances as a threat to their own self-interest.

Final Comments

The poor organizational care of such institutions as the state hospital is a testimony to our past failures in mental health treatment. Similarly, we have found that when the target population for care are the ones who are showing gross symptoms, we are admitting the failure of the mental health system to become involved in early prevention and intervention approaches which might have avoided having the patients present now in such a state of advanced distress. Furthermore, the past revolutions in mental health have exhibited a failure to utilize manpower effectively and have indicated a move in the direction of further solidifying self-interests for status and financial reasons. In essence, the past history of mental health is not a pleasant one.

Yet, despite these failures and short-sighted moves on the part of those who claimed the responsibility for the care of the emotionally disturbed, the previous stages were necessary. Though sometimes progress was held off or diverted by the very people who spearheaded mental health treatment and research, the steps previous to today's human services movement have created an increasing environment of concern for the emotional welfare for others, and for this we must be grateful.

REFERENCES

Beigal, Allan and Levenson, Alan (Eds.): *The Community Mental Health Center.* Basic Books, New York, 1972.

Deutsch, A.: *The Mentally Ill in America.* Columbia Univ. Press, New York, 1946.

Panzetta, Anthony F.: *Community Mental Health: Myth and Reality.* Lea & Febiger, Philadelphia, 1971.

Whittington, H. G.: *Clinical Practice in Community Mental Health Centers.* International Universities Press, New York, 1972.

Chapter 2

COMMUNITY MENTAL HEALTH: MILESTONES IN THE UNITED STATES

Bold current concepts and actions in modern community mental health are but one step in an overall historical process. What the future holds is always questionable; one can only speculate. The past history of the mental health movement in the United States, on the other hand, is marked by certain distinct milestones which can be traced.

These historical markers are important for at least two obvious reasons: They illustrate how the management of emotional problems were interrelated with the philosophies of the times. For example, how did military psychiatry differ in quality and approach during World Wars I and II? Answers to questions like this one are possible by looking back at past policy.

The milestones also help us see how mental health policy and action developed in the United States. Such information not only points to where the human services movement is now, but also gives some indication as to where it might possibly be going in the future.

Since the interest in this book is centered on the evolution and present features of the human services movement, attention will be paid particularly to the antecedents of the *community* mental health movement in the United States. Such historical markers will include those occurrences or developments that professionals in the mental health field generally consider to have had a profound impact on current public policy (Mechanic 1969; Weston 1976; Yolles 1975).

Dorothea Dix (1802–1887)

If there ever was a character in the mental health movement whose work can truly be considered to have had an ironic outcome, it was the efforts made on behalf of Dorothea Dix after her death, for contained in her good work in the mid 1800s were the seeds of a subsequently disastrous mental health policy.

Ms. Dix's efforts were directed at ensuring that the mentally ill received humane treatment, that the hell-holes used to confine the seriously emotionally disturbed were eliminated. Her dedication to the goal of eliminating situations in which a disturbed person received little or no treatment or was punished instead of helped was paralleled only by the influence she amassed among those in powerful positions.

The key elements she felt to correcting the current ills of the present custody system was the creation of clean, modern, pleasant, and restful facilities where patients would be assured of good treatment. The problem with this approach, though, is that it assumed that the nation as a whole would continue to monitor and support progress in these institutions. She felt that with the proper public pressure and financial support, these facilities would not turn out to be the dungeons of the past—as in pre-Pinel France. As we know, her assumptions proved quite faulty.

The first fatal blow to her plans was the veto of 1854 in which the federal government threw the financial responsibilities for the care of the mentally ill back to the states. In other words, it would be the states who would be tasked with paying for institutional treatment and the construction of new facilities. This loss of federal revenue, the growing apathy of the public in matters of overseeing institutional policy, and the advent of the industrial revolution, which resulted in accelerated use of hospitalization for those who could not cope (Grob 1966), led to overcrowding and poor care.

What started out as a seemingly good idea to Dorothea Dix ended up in the development of a system of tragedy—a collection of massive, lonely, understaffed, overutilized fortresses for the mentally ill. The state institution is only now beginning to finally be supplanted—to a large degree—by community alternatives. For too long the institution stood as a block to progress in mental health. Unfortunately, as in much of the mental health movement, it started out with the zeal of someone who sought change for the better, but produced instead a less desirable result in the end.

National Association for Mental Health (NAMH)—1909

Citizen involvement in mental health policy was given an organized forum in 1909 in the creation of the National Association for Mental Health. This association was given its life mainly through the work and writings of one person—Clifford Beers.

Like Dorothea Dix, who was a teacher, Beers was a well-educated person who was not professionally involved in psychology/psychiatry. However, whereas Ms. Dix's work was an outgrowth of her contact with female offenders in 1841 as a Sunday school teacher, Beers efforts came about after his experiences as a three-time mental patient.

In 1905, Beers—a Yale graduate—published *A Mind That Found Itself*. In it he reports his own recovery in a compassionate attendant's house and the inhumane treatment he received in three different institutions. In 1908 Beers added to the impact of the publication of his book by founding the Connecticut Society for Mental Hygiene. This small organization was eventually to lead to the formation of a larger private national association, the National Association for Mental Health. Though their initial impact on public policy was modest, these groups have grown in numbers and in power. Today, they represent a notable voice in the private sector concerning the care of the emotionally troubled and seriously disturbed.

World Wars I and II: Military Psychiatry

Military psychiatry during the First World War demonstrated clearly the fact that knowing what to do and doing it are two quite different things. As early as July 18, 1918, General John J. Pershing asked for better screening of troops for mental fitness prior to sending them overseas for action.

In response to this request, Doctors Thomas Salmon, Taliaferro Clark, and Walter Treadway initiated early recognition and crisis intervention methods here in the states. Though short of personnel, they did their best to eliminate obviously mentally unfit troops, i.e. psychotic, retarded, and provide treatment to as many as possible through short term and group-oriented approaches.

Out of their experiences came the development of a plan of action which included recommendations for the following:

1. Psychiatric screening of recruits.
2. Immediate short term treatment as close to the line as possible.
3. In the case of necessity, further treatment facilities at base, debarkation, and embarkation points.
4. Psychiatric training in military hospitals and at the division level.
5. Discharge for the mentally retarded.

This plan—developed at the end of World War I—showed that, given the problem, the military psychiatric personnel could meet it, if enough personnel and attention to the plan were provided. However, after World War I, the plan was buried in a surgeon general's report for almost twenty years without any significant action taken on it!

World War II saw the acceptance and utilization of more untraditional but useful short term and group approaches. Also, the war brought to the fore again the fact that there was a great shortage of mental health professionals in the military. For example, in a recruit depot, it was not unusual for a psychiatrist to be required to see 200 men per day. Furthermore, World War II made the public more aware of the potential magnitude of mental problems of the nation's people. Over $1\frac{3}{4}$ million men were rejected for reasons involving mental health alone!

National Institute of Mental Health (NIMH)

With the recognition of the critical problems in the mental health care of the people of the United States put out in the open by World War II rejection statistics, Congress acted by passing the *Mental Health Act of 1946*. As a result of this act, the National Institute of Mental Health was given life.

The NIMH was assigned the task of helping the states develop mental health training, research, and personnel development program guidelines. Helping to formulate prevention and public education was also left to them. Though initially only a small agency, its original budget has continued to grow, thus demonstrating an increased financial investment in this area (see Table I).

In 1946, the NIMH's total budget represented only 2½ million dollars, despite the wide ranging mandate it received from Congress "to improve the mental health of the people of the United States." In 1973, the NIMH budget was 700 million dollars. Today, it is a key agency for mental health under the federal government's authority.

TABLE 2-I

BUDGETS OF THE NATIONAL INSTITUTE OF MENTAL HEALTH

Year	Budget (In millions of dollars)
1973	$700
1967	$338
1960	$ 68
1950	$ 9
1946	$ 2.5

Action for Mental Health—1961

Following the *Mental Health Act of 1946,* on both state and federal levels there came about a heightened interest in the plight of the institutionalized patient and a deep concern for those seeking help but, for lack of services, unable to get it.

In 1955 Congress passed the *Mental Health Study Act* and provided funding for the *Joint Commission on Mental Illness and Health.* The authority was given to this commission with the hope that it could find some solution to the personnel shortage in the mental health field. Establishment of the commission was predicated further on the belief that state hospitals were not working. Finally, there was a growing belief that alternatives to institutionalization were not only possible, but quite necessary.

A further and underlying goal of the commission was to provide an overall general impression of the extent of the nation's mental illness problems and the care currently available to deal with them. The outcome of this study was revealed in a final report published in 1961 under the title of *Action for Mental Health.*

The findings were as expected, but somehow their impact was still strongly felt by the President, the Congress, and the public. Generally, they found mental health care to be woefully inadequate and fragmented. As well as personnel shortages, there was a significant lack of coordination among what services were available.

To correct this situation, they recommended such steps as:

1. Increased utilization of mental health workers through improved recruitment and training.
2. Added funds for mental health, i.e. current expenditures to be tripled in ten years.
3. New programs for both acute and chronically ill patients in mental health clinics, general hospitals, and in residential facilities for the emotionally disturbed.
4. Provisions for aftercare for mentally ill persons.
5. Establishment of new mental health clinics to provide comprehensive and continuous care in the open community.
6. Improved research facilities to study mental health and illness; added funds would be provided to support this pursuit.

Community Mental Health Centers Act—1963

Action for Mental Health was well received and acted on quickly and positively for a number of reasons. Among them were (Mechanic 1969, p. 60) :

1. A healthy economy.
2. A president especially interested in issues involving mental health/mental retardation.
3. Increased recognition that institutionalization wasn't working.
4. Recognition that psychotropic drugs, i.e. antipsychotic ones like chlorpromazine (Thorazine®) and minor tranquillizers like diazepam (Valium®), could enable disturbed people to remain in the community while undergoing treatment.
5. A wide ranging rejection of the status quo of mental health

care which previously ignored the poor and catered only to those who could afford private treatment.

Consequently, when President Kennedy put forth a plan for an innovative approach to the nation's mental health ills, Congress expedited the requested legislation and passed the *Community Mental Health Center's Act of 1963*. This document was clearly a sign that public policy in the delivery of mental health care would take on a new direction. The National Institute of Mental Health under the supervision of the U.S. Department of Health, Education, and Welfare would provide guidance to all levels of government who wished to participate in this new approach.

A main element in this act, for which the NIMH would set up regulations and requirements for funding, was the establishment of community mental health centers. These newly designed centers were proposed as a means to offer new, diverse, multipurpose settings to service both the poor and economically well-off. In the past fifteen years, in the process of the states and local communities affecting changes and innovations to qualify for funding for such centers, the complexion of the community mental health scene has radically changed. It is within this altered environment that the modern human services movement, with its utilization of creative, short term, and group-oriented approaches, along with the application of nonprofessional workers, has flourished.

Final Comments

Community mental health proponents still wonder today about the condition the treatment system might be in if it were not for the timing of actions by such key figures as President Kennedy and Dorothea Dix. Both were influenced by good motives; both proposed radical moves. The latter diverted the ultimate path of community mental health temporarily; the former accelerated it.

Whatever the outcome might have been, however, is left for the philosophers to ponder. The fact is we are now faced with an era of new technologies and manpower utilization. Before we can fully evaluate the community mental health program and offer suggestions for change, we must appreciate it for what it is—a significant move in a new direction to provide greater quality care for the people in the community who need it.

REFERENCES

Grob, G.: *The State and the Mentally Ill.* Univ. of North Carolina Press, Chapel Hill, North Carolina, 1966.

Mechanic, David: *Mental Health and Social Policy.* Prentice-Hall, Englewood Cliffs, New Jersey, 1969.

Weston, W. Donald: Development of community psychiatry concepts. In Freedman, Alfred M., Kaplan, Harold I., and Sadock, Benjamin J. (Eds.): *Comprehensive Textbook of Psychiatry.* Vol. 2. Williams & Wilkins, Baltimore, 1976.

Yolles, Stanley F.: Community psychiatry: 1963-1974. Paper presented at the Missouri Institute of Psychiatry, St. Louis, April 1975.

PART II

MODERN MENTAL HEALTH
TECHNOLOGY

Chapter 3

MODERN STRATEGIES OF INTERVENTION IN THE HUMAN SERVICES*

THOUGH THE COMMUNITY mental health movement is representative of the fourth revolution in mental health, it is only one indication of the whole new philosophy of treatment now present. The human services model is based on a number of tenets which are in variance with the medical model.

MEDICAL MODEL

The *medical model* is based on a number of premises. Essentially, they are as follows:

1. A person who seeks for a mental disturbance should be treated as a *patient*.

2. The patient is considered to be sick; this sickness is considered to be viewed as a disease.

3. The therapist's first aim is to diagnose the disease entity so that a specific treatment can be designated to deal with it.

4. In cases not directly involving some physical organic etiology, the cause is relegated to some inner (intrapsychic) disequilibrium in the personality.

5. In treating the patient, the therapist must correct this unconscious problem for the difficulty to be alleviated.

6. The "talking treatment," utilized to help the person handle his problem, is directed usually at increasing this individual's understanding of it. To afford such insight the therapist focuses on the interpersonal and intrapsychic material that comes up in the session.

7. Except in the case of serious disturbances (psychosis), the patient is only dealt with in the context of the therapy hour and not outside of the therapy room.

---

*See also Appendices 1-3.

8. The therapist provides verbal guidance, and active corrective work is delegated to the patient; it is the person who comes to treatment who is expected to affect change within himself and the environment.

Medical Model: An Illustration

To appreciate the contrast between the medical and human services models, an illustration of how the medical model is put into effect will be provided before moving on to a coverage of the human services model.

Presenting Complaint: Thirty-four-year-old male complains of chronic, low-level depression.

Diagnosis: Doctor does a diagnostic work-up. This includes a careful evaluation of the person's mental status, a full history of the complaint, and an extremely thorough background history.

Therapeutic Agreement: A decision is made regarding the patient's acceptance into treatment, the type of treatment the patient needs, and the frequency he will be coming for therapy sessions. In this case, the patient is tentatively diagnosed as a neurotic depressive. His treatment is designated as insight-oriented psychoanalytic psychotherapy. (The therapist will attempt to get the patient to see the connection between his present situation and occurrences in his early life; the belief is that once insight is attained and integrated within the personality, change will be possible.) The patient will be expected to come twice per week; the fee is fifty dollars per session.

HUMAN SERVICES MODEL

Though the above approach may prove quite effective with a verbal, relatively young, intelligent, upper middle-income person, it would not meet the needs of much of the current population coming for help. This became obvious when the statistics started showing that such traditional treatment based on the medical model resulted in—

1. An increasing number of patients going untreated because of a lack in the patient's wealth, intelligence, or ability to undergo long term treatment.

2. An overcrowding in the state hospitals because of the unavailability of treatment for those who wanted it, and the ineffectiveness of the traditional methods with those who received it.

Accordingly, with the movement away from the sickness model supported by statistics showing its ineffectiveness with much of the population, and an increasing recognition of the faults of the medical model on the part of such psychiatric pioneers as Doctors Maxwell Jones (1952), Thomas Szasz (1961), and Erich Lindemann (1944), to name but a few, the human services model came into wider use. Though this model can vary a great deal from setting to setting, there are a number of characteristics which, for the most part, reflect its essential core:

1. A person seeking help is looked upon as a client.

2. The client's behavior is seen as maladaptive rather than sick; thus, efforts are taken with the person to replace this behavior with a more effective repertoire.

3. Rather than being separated from his family, home, job, and community, every effort is made to keep/retie the connections. This is accomplished by involving the family in the treatment, treating the person in the community (rather than in an isolated hospital), attacking the symptoms first, dealing with current problems, and intervening when necessary in the environment to find or tap existing resources to assist the client during this and future stressful periods.

4. The personnel used to assist the client come from varied backgrounds and educational levels.

5. Social ills i.e. unemployment, and concrete problems, such as sickness in the family, are handled directly while intrapsychic problems are generally not dealt with, except in rare cases.

Crisis Intervention

A good illustration of a method of therapeutic intervention is possible to see by looking at an example of crisis intervention.

Crisis intervention is one term that can be used to describe a whole series of recently introduced, brief treatment techniques employing a wide variety of personnel, service organizations, auspices, and formal labels. Crisis intervention includes, for example, suicide prevention services using telephone and in-person interviews, teen-age counseling as offered through "hot line" and "drop-in centers," pastoral counseling, brief psychotherapy offered in emergency "walk-in clinics," family dispute intervention provided by specially trained policemen, window-to-window programs, and a host of similar programs. (Zusman 1975, P. 2335)

Crisis intervention can be differentiated from the more traditional, long term therapeutic modalities by the following unique characteristics:

1. The goal of crisis intervention is to re-establish the link between the client and his/her environment as quickly as possible. As a result, the primary focus is on the observable difficulties, not the deep-seated ones; furthermore, the family and the community (agencies, place of employment, religious organization of client) are actively involved in the treatment.

2. The treatment provided is time-limited. The aim is to provide the client and other significant persons involved so that long term treatment is not necessary. Positive results are sought in the shortest time possible so long term disengagement with the environment does not result.

3. A firm relationship with the therapist is *discouraged*. Dependency and attachment to a single helper is avoided. Rather, a team of workers are assigned to each case so that the client's problem, and not the person, is the area of focus. Also, the normal supports in a person's life (family, friends) are used so reattachment to them is cemented; the belief is that the establishment of a relationship with the treatment agency only serves to further sever past ties, which is deemed undesirable.

4. The waiting period for treatment is kept short, and efforts are made to intervene before a debilitating pattern develops. Quick medical, psychological, and social evaluations are performed by the physicians, nurses, community workers, psychologists, social workers, and other staff members. Immediately after evaluation, multimodal treatment is offered by

the entire staff; community intervention by an indigenous paraprofessional is deemed just as important as medical support by a physician.

Crisis Intervention: An Illustration

A man, forty-one years of age, lost the job he had been workat for fifteen years.   Immediately following this loss, he became very depressed and, instead of looking for another job, started drinking heavily.   Then, three weeks after being laid off, he attempted suicide by crashing his car into a tree.

During his hospital stay, no mention was made of the attempt by him or his wife.   However, soon after his release, his wife became frightened that he would try again, his drinking having increased once more.   Feeling this way, she convinced him to seek help at the local community mental health center's crisis unit.

The immediate evaluation was conducted by a psychiatric nurse.   She felt that suicide was indeed a serious possibility if the depression and excessive drinking were not curbed.   A medical consultation was sought to see if antidepressive drugs might not be of help; a team meeting was also scheduled for the same day to plan interventions, since antidepressives take several days to three weeks to take effect.   Also, a decision would have to be reached as to whether hospitalization would be required.

At this meeting, the problems leading up to the crisis were traced (see Fig. 3-1).   Once this was accomplished, a plan was developed and acted upon by the team in conjunction with the patient, his family, and the community.

- Loss of job
- Disequilibrium caused by sudden absence of occupational role, financial support, and activity which occupied last fifteen years of life
- Feelings of worthlessness
- Depression and anxiety
- Inability to conduct problem solving activity
- Alcoholic intake to alleviate pain caused by depression and anxiety
- Family pressures because of job loss and increased drinking
- Added alcoholic intake and increased feelings of hopelessness and helplessness

CRISIS

- Suicide attempt

Figure 3-1. Outline of a crisis situation.

Plan: A mental health worker, an employment consultant and a social worker met with the patient, his wife, and their two children. The client was encouraged to discuss how he had gotten his previous job, what his duties were, how he felt about it, and if he had ever thought leaving it would be to his advantage. Then he was encouraged to speak about the feelings he had about being laid off and the way he felt his family and others viewed his job loss.

After these feelings were brought out in the open, his family was asked to respond. Once this was done, the employment consultant was asked to recommend what might be done to seek a new position. He said that a meeting with the client would be set up for the next day to go over other employment opportunities and to discuss retraining. The social worker indicated that social service support and unemployment applications would be filed in the interim. The mental health worker suggested between five to eight meetings with the family to talk over the upheaval and their reactions to the efforts to readjust to the problems.

In the final session with the mental health worker, there was a discussion of how the family was getting along on unemployment payments, what the client thought of his new job training program, and how the client felt about his current situation.

Though immediate progress had been made and the imminent threat of suicide was passed, the crisis team felt follow-up by someone in the client's community mental health center would be warranted. Consequently, the family was referred to the client's catchment area clinic for more long term counseling; in addition, one more meeting was set up with the family's clergyman so that they could turn to someone for help in their own community circle after treatment was terminated in the clinic.

Crisis intervention is meant as a quick remedy to a dangerous situation. It is not long term; therapists are not passive; the team is interdisciplinary; and the community is drawn in as is the family to aid in the treatment. Such a short term approach which emphasizes active intervention is usually quite effective and can be used in many settings with a plethora of crisis situations. With problem solving techniques, the team gets everyone—including the client—to attack the problem. The process is interesting to observe and to be involved in, as well as to read about in the texts now available on the topic (Aguilera et al. 1975; Lieb et al. 1973; Wicks 1977).

NEW CAREERS MOVEMENT

Human services in the 1960s was characterized by one general, pervading theme, namely, that *everyone* (including the poor and unemployed) has a right to know what resources exist in the community, to have access to them as clients and workers, and to be involved in the creative expansion of current services. This meant that all community members should have the opportunity to participate in the planning and supervision of community mental health centers and other service agencies. The thrust of the new human services movement also included an emphasis on the creation of new careers and roles for *paraprofessionals.**

*The term "paraprofessional" is looked upon by some as being pedantic. However, since it and similar terms (associate professional, nonprofessional, new careerist, new professional, indigenous worker) have not been replaced by a better term, and they are still widely used in the literature, they will be used in this book to differentiate those workers in new roles and careers not already covered by an existing professional group, i.e. American Psychological Association, National Association of Social Workers, American Psychiatric Association.

Prior to the 1960s there were some positions for nonprofessionals, but they usually were limited to closed roles with little authority. A good example of this was the psychiatric aide title. Though open to nonprofessionals, this job was a road to nowhere. Promotion was not possible. Training was practically nonexistent, and the salary was low. Moreover, there was little appreciation on the part of the salaried professionals or the important effect such workers have through their daily contact with the population being served. Also, little effort was made to recruit from the pool of unemployed, low-income residents available.

To the contrary, the new careers movement meant the development of career ladders, with the chance for upward mobility for the previously untrained, uneducated, disenfranchised, and unemployed. It also involved special efforts to recruit indigenous workers, i.e. people who were from the very areas where most of the clients were coming from for help.

This new cadre of paraprofessionals were not attached to service agencies to be "re-educated, professionalized, and brainwashed into accepting middle-class mores." Rather, they were recruited so they could offer their unique viewpoints and talents as community members who were in close connection with the client population to be served.

The paraprofessionals were not trained to just replace the professionals in some of their duties, but were encouraged to expand the discontinuous, far-from-comprehensive, traditional services that were previously available. As outreach workers, they were assigned to make people aware of new services now existent in each neighborhood. As direct service personnel, they were expected to be involved in a vast array of interpersonal activities. As supervisory and planning staff members, they were given the chance to share in the responsibility of ensuring that the new careers movement in the area actually worked.

In the spirit of community psychiatry, one of the overriding objectives of employing paraprofessionals was to help adapt public health practice to the field of mental health. In this vein, the hope was that the new professionals could improve the quality of care for community members by:

1. Increasing the scope of services available.
2. Providing assistance close to the homes of the clients.
3. Actively securing participation of clients and their families not only in their own treatment, but via their roles as communication facilitators in the community to help attract others who were in need of help.

On primary, secondary, and tertiary prevention levels, the paraprofessionals were given opportunities to make an impact (see Fig. 3-2). The overall significance and size of the new careers

---

Primary Prevention—Preventative efforts directed at reducing the *incidence* of new instances of emotional disturbances:

1. Be advocates of social and environmental improvement.
2. Encourage social agencies (community mental health, criminal justice) to be more responsive to the needs of the people.
3. Reduce the chances of people in crisis becoming long-term clients through the provision of emergency counseling.

Secondary Prevention—Efforts made to reduce the *length* of an emotional disturbance:

1. Be involved in early detection procedures so that immediate referral is possible.
2. Educate the public as to what services are available in the community.
3. Assist in planning the development of human services resources close to the community being served.

Tertiary Prevention—Efforts taken to reduce an emotional disorder's long-term effect:

1. Assist in the assessment, training, and placement of clients in educational/occupational positions where they can increase independence and self-respect.
2. Support the clients' efforts to re-establish links with their families and the community.

Figure 3-2. Nonprofessionals and prevention in mental health: illustrations of their roles in primary, secondary, and tertiary prevention.

movement can not then be underplayed. Today it has literally grasped one of the most important positions in the human services movement.

New Careers Concept

"New careers" was coined as a new term in the book published by Arthur Pearl and Frank Reissman in 1965. This volume, *New Careers for the Poor: The Nonprofessional in Human Services,* described the theme of the *new* paraprofessional movement as they saw it.

> The new career concept has as a point of departure the creation of jobs normally allotted to highly trained professionals or technicians, but which could be performed by the unskilled, inexperienced, and relatively untrained worker; or, the development of activities not currently performed by anyone, but for which there is a readily acknowledged need and which can also be satisfactorily accomplished by the unskilled worker. (P. 13)

The mid-1960s was the time when the new careers movement got its major push. Though the actual employment of nonprofessionals can be traced back earlier, it was during this period that a stress was put on the use of *indigenous paraprofessionals* and the *development of career ladders for nonprofessionals.*

Indigenous Nonprofessionals

The new careers movement came about at a time when certain classes of people (ones in specific age, racial, geographical categories) were being turned out of their jobs. Their exclusion from the occupational work force was highlighted by the fact that unemployment at the time was not high in all classes.

This trend toward high unemployment and occupational dislocation among certain groups was highlighted in a number of books (Levine 1968; Harrington 1962). They helped provide the philosophy for the push to employ indigenous personnel and added to some of the other existing motives for utilizing them.

The paraprofessional movement at large included recommendations to hire the middle class nonprofessional (referred to by Reiff and Riessman, 1964, as the "ubiquitous nonprofessional") as well as ones residing in the geographical area in which most of the clients are located. However, the support for utilizing indigenous nonprofessionals was that, in addition to extending the work of professionals, which the ubiquitous nonprofessional could do, the indigenous nonprofessional could also

1. Provide a conduit to the community at large.

2. Make the professional services more relevant to a community where the mores and lifestyles may be different.

3. Fill meaningful positions rather than remain on the unemployment roles.

4. Be a future source of indigenous supervisors.

Accordingly, because of their potential value, program administrators and planners have been taking steps to attract indigenous workers—ones who, according to Grosser's definition (1969), "reside in the target area, engage in social, economic and political processes similar to those of program participants, and are matched with them on such characteristics as social class, race, ethnicity, religion, language, culture, and mores" (p. 123).

Career Ladder for Nonprofessionals

One of the other key features of the new careers approach to modern human services involves the development of opportunities for advancement for nonprofessionals. Prior to the 1960s those paraprofessional positions open were usually dead-end positions. With the legislation and books on the movement supporting changes in this, the new jobs created were entry level positions.

Instead of a person coming in and getting the title of psychiatric aide, the nonprofessional could qualify for a job title such as mental health worker trainee. With this role came the promise of future training and the opportunity to move up the paraprofessional ranks to new roles (supervisory and principal mental health worker titles) and greater responsibilities which carried with them higher salaries. In some cases, there was even an opportunity to continue formal education and move into the professional ranks, for example as a psychologist or social worker.

Final Comments

The human services movement today has many facets. The creative intervention methods and the new careers movement provide the main elements of the change in health strategies brought on with great fervor in the middle of the twentieth century.

Long term therapy reserved for the wealthy and state institutions comprising the bulk of the health services for the emotionally disturbed among the poor were attacked in the 1950s and 1960s. In the place of the traditional modalities, new methods of intervention and better facilities in the community from which service could be provided to all people were established.

The impact of the legislation as well as the new programs that it supported, was felt in the areas of mental health particularly, since there was a great emphasis not only to establish community mental health centers, but also to staff them with a new cadre of paraprofessionals and volunteers.

Though they did not provide a complete, pat answer to the mental health problems of the community, community mental health centers—at the very least—turned the health system around. They did demonstrate that innovation and multilevel personnel can be something special for a care delivery system. With this in mind, the next two chapters will be devoted to a look at new professionals and volunteers in mental health.

REFERENCES

Aguilera, Donna C. and Messick, Janice M.: *Crisis Intervention: Theory and Methodology.* Mosby, St. Louis, 1974.

Grosser, C. F.: Manpower development programs. In Grosser, C. F., Henry, W. E., and Kelly, J. G. (Eds.): *Nonprofessionals in the Human Services.* Jossey-Bass, San Francisco, 1969.

Harrington, M. *The Other American: Poverty in the United States.* Macmillan, New York, 1962.

Jones, Maxwell, McGee, R., and Grant, J.: *Social Psychiatry.* Tavistock Publications, London, 1952.

Levine, L.: The antecedents of our currently changing manpower assets. In *Poverty and Human Resources Abstracts.* Vol. 3. Jan-Feb., 1968.

Lieb, Julian, Lipsitch, Ian I., and Slaby, Andrew Edmund: *The Crisis Team: A Handbook for the Mental Health Professional.* Harper &

Row, New York, 1973.

Lindemann, Erich: Symptomatology and management of acute grief. *American Journal of Psychiatry, 101,* 141, 1944.

Pearl, A. and Reissman, F.: *New Careers for the Poor: The Nonprofessional in Human Services.* Free Press, New York, 1965.

Reiff, R. and Reissman, F.: *The Indigenous Nonprofessional: A Strategy of Change in Community Action and Community Mental Health Programs.* National Institute of Labor Education, New York, 1964.

Szasz, T.: *The Myth of Mental Illness.* Harper & Row, New York, 1961.

Wicks, R.: *Counseling Strategies and Intervention Techniques for the Human Services.* Lippincott, Philadelphia, 1977.

Zusman, J.: Secondary prevention. In Freedman, A., Kaplan, H., and Sadock, B. (Eds.): *Comprehensive Textbook of Psychiatry.* Vol. 2. Williams & Wilkins, Baltimore, 1976.

Chapter 4

NEW CAREERS AND ROLES
IN MENTAL HEALTH*

G EORGE W. ALBEE WAS A REALIST in the assessment of manpower
needs he presented in a study for the Joint Commission on
Mental Illness and Health in 1959. There was a *crisis*. His recognition that professionals alone would never be able to provide
complete care to a majority of the people was quite sound.

Following his report and additional input from other key
leaders in the new careers and paraprofessional movements, legislation and new programs were initiated to spur a new drive for
better mental health care. While there were many elements of
the Community Mental Health Movement, Great Society programs, and Anti-Poverty projects, one of the key aspects was the
push for the development of new careers and roles in mental
health.

Initially, the hope was that nonprofessionals (including indigenous personnel) could be trained to support the work of existing professionals. However, as the programs formed, they fostered
greater hopes, for as salaried and volunteer paraprofessionals became involved in institutional and community mental health
work, a number of more ambitious results were seen as attainable.

In those instances where new personnel were not blocked from
employing their talents, this additional source of manpower was
often able to:

1. Establish innovative services not previously offered by
the center or institution at which they worked.

2. Reach populations not previously thought amenable to
mental health services.

3. Provide a new source of leadership and supervisory personnel, as well as assist in the direct service roles for which
they were originally hired.

*See also Appendices 4 and 5.

36

4. Bring new realizations of the social and cultural supports that a health agency can offer, if the helping agent is aware of the mores and lifestyles of the community being served.

With the dawning of the 1960s and the movement to establish new careers and roles in mental health, there was hope then that new help was on the way. As was mentioned earlier in the book, new stresses were on the poor stemming from such pressures as high unemployment due to increased industrialization and the demand for one to possess specialized, advanced training to get a decent, stable position in the work force. Simultaneously, there was an increased awareness and militancy on the part of the socially and financially oppressed to get help, both in the form of jobs and training, as well as in terms of better, more responsive human services.

The time was right then during the beginning of the Kennedy Presidency for a major experiment in the utilization of new types of workers in creative roles. Consequently, major efforts were made to explore different uses for paraprofessionals, and, in turn, to develop added ways to recruit, train, assimilate, and accredit the increased influx of these untraditional human services personnel.

EMPLOYING MENTAL HEALTH PARAPROFESSIONALS

Utilization of new professionals in mental health has varied from setting to setting according to the innovativeness of the professionals and paraprofessionals on staff and the limits placed by agency and governmental policy. Despite this variance among programs, though, there have been a number of attempts to provide general categories for the types of functions nonprofessionals normally perform.

Francine Sobey, in a National Institute of Mental Health survey, for example, presented the following classification based on her observations of existing methods of nonprofessional utilization:

- the caretaking function, which includes the provision of physical care and supervision as, for example, in institutional care, or foster homes, or by a homemaker;
- the bridging function, which helps make the connection between the

person in need and sources of help through interpreting, expediting, and linking activities;

- the sustenance, or social support, function which may be provided through "substitutive personal relationships"; and

- the *professional assistant* function, i.e. serving as an aide, or assistant, and functioning in a closely adjunctive manner to the professional, and under his direct supervision; this may include counseling activity approaching professional therapeutic intervention. (Sobey 1969, P. 15)

Categorizing the roles of mental health workers and other psychiatric assistants in terms of "tasks performed," however, can be quite misleading. There is much overlap in the types of activities performed by paraprofessionals. Furthermore, even a single task can be done for different reasons—thus changing the objective of the paraprofessional performing it.

For instance, if a mental health trainee plays a game of checkers with a patient on a hospital ward to see how dexterous the person is in fine motor coordination and how good the patient's current interpersonal skills are, he is serving as an evaluator. If the same game is played with the purpose of building up rapport with the patient so that a therapeutic relationship can be established, the trainee's role is one of counselor.

With this distinction in mind, a number of specialists on the subject of the mental health worker's role definition (McPheeters, King and Teare 1972) decided to view the paraprofessional's roles in a different manner. They saw the roles in terms of "a set of alternative activities or functions that might be performed to meet a common objective" (p. 330).

They saw roles in terms of being possibly different facets of an overall job. With this schema in mind, they designated a number of roles which the mental health worker might fill at different times, though the title might not reflect the specific duties involved in performing them. These roles include the following:

- *Outreach worker:* reaches out into the community to detect people with problems, help them find assistance, and follow up to ensure that their needs are being met.

- *Broker:* helps individuals or families get needed services. This role involves assessing situations, knowing about resources, counseling the client, contracting the appropriate resources, and making sure that the client gets to it and receives services.

- *Advocate:* pleads and fights for services for a single client whom the system would otherwise reject or for changes in laws, regulations, and practices for the benefit of a class of clients.
- *Evaluator:* gathers information, assesses client or community problems, weighs alternatives and sets priorities, and makes decisions for action.
- *Teacher:* teaches subjects ranging from simple things such as how to dress or plan a meal to more complex material.
- *Behavior Changer:* carries out a range of activities directed at changing an individual's behavior. They include simple coaching, counseling, and use of behavior modification techniques.
- *Mobilizer:* works to develop new facilities, resources, and programs and to make them available to people who are not being served.
- *Consultant:* works with individuals to help them increase their skills and with agencies to help them in solving their clients' problems.
- *Community planner:* assists neighborhood and community groups and agencies in planning programs to meet human service needs.
- *Caregiver:* gives supportive services to people who are not able to resolve their problems fully and meet their own needs. The caregiver may provide supportive counseling, fiscal support, protective services, day care, or twenty-four-hour care.
- *Data manager:* gathers, tabulates, analyzes, and synthesizes data needed for making decisions and taking action. The work ranges from gathering case data and preparing simple statistical reports of program activities to conducting program evaluation and sophisticated research.
- *Administrator:* performs all the activities directed toward planning and carrying out a program. They include planning, personnel work, budget and fiscal management, and supervision. (McPheeters, King, and Teare 1972, Pp, 330-331)

Though specific programs may provide different examples of how a mental health nonprofessional is used in each case, the roles listed can be subsumed under one of the above headings. As is true to the human services model, however, in a majority of cases most of the time spent by mental health workers is in *action*-oriented pursuits. While it is true that administrative and planning roles are filled by paraprofessionals, it is their ability to reach out and understand the community that has made the paraprofessional movement so important.

For instance, when a Youth Worker Project was established in Toronto General Hospital in 1971 (Robinson and Alboim 1974), its primary goal was to increase communication with the youthful patient. To accomplish this they hired five youths to do the following:

> 1. Staff the emergency department from 9:00 PM to 3:00 AM, assisting in the care of young people, especially drug-hurt youth.
> 2. Follow up, upon admission or discharge either from the emergency department or from the hospital proper, all youths who desired such service.
> 3. Establish liaisons with all youth-serving agencies and other services.
> 4. Assist in the development of an in-service education program (Robinson and Alboim 1974, P. 469).

Another aspect in the mental health paraprofessional movement that is significant is the fascinating as well as complex roles the new careerist is now filling in some settings. One of these new roles is the interesting work paraprofessionals are involved in with very disturbed patients (schizophrenics, psychotics).

In one instance a therapeutic assistant was used to assist in aiding a schizophrenic to become reattached to the external world (Arieti and Lorraine 1972). The assistant became actively involved with the patient, which a therapist could not do because of time considerations. She also provided another healthy relationship for the patient to become involved with during the treatment until such time that other relationships could be formed. Also, the use of a therapeutic assistant helped ensure continuity in the treatment. If the primary therapist had to discontinue therapy, the assistant could provide an unbroken link.

Another illustration of a similar, but logical, study which utilized aides with very seriously disturbed patients was reported by Doctors Edward Shelley and Ronald R. Fieve (1974). They discussed the findings of an attempt to use non-physicians (nurses and aides in teams) in a health maintenance program for affective disorders, i.e. manic-depressive illness, which is a marked mood disturbance. Each of the persons involved in the study was being treated with a special drug, Lithium®. This drug is usually given to manic-depressive patients, and must be monitored to ensure effectiveness and to avoid inappropriate side reactions.

> The 20 patients studied had all been followed for the same 78-week period, during which they were seen and interviewed at least once a month by teams of psychiatric nurses and aides. The teams used a manic-depressive rating scale to detect symptoms that might need a physician's attention. Fourteen of the patients remained free of affective episodes and never required the services of a psychiatrist. The approach expanded the availability of psychiatric services without sacrificing effectiveness. (P. 303)

In one report on the use of nonprofessionals with persons suffering from acute episodes who were being treated in a house in the community, the professionals involved claims that the new worker can be at a natural advantage over his traditional counterparts.

> We believe that relatively untrained, psychologically unsophisticated persons can work within this theoretical framework more easily than highly trained ones because they have learned no theory of schizophrenic . . . . this allows them freedom to be themselves, to follow visceral responses, to adapt a phenomenological stance, and to be a "person" with the psychotic individual. (Mosher, Reifman, and Menn 1973, P. 391)

The title of "broker" is another position that a new careerist can ideally fill in the community mental health center. The broker's role is similar to two others that are currently filled by mental health workers in various community centers. These titles are the "enabler" and the "advocate."

An enabler "is concerned with improving the operational procedures and adding services . . . with improving the efficiency of the existing system of delivery of services" (Spergel 1969). The advocate, on the other hand, is someone who is exclusively allied with the clients and their interests. This person operates with the belief that improved links with the community—which will lead to better utilization of human services—requires the presence of someone who will lead the legal and technical attack on institutions that are not responsive enough to the clients' needs.

The broker is slightly different in terms of the role definition it carries, according to Ricky Dancy, a social research assistant at the Mecklenburg County Mental Health Center in Charlotte, North Carolina.

> The broker, somewhere between those two extremes (enabler and advocate), serves as a guide and a liaison. He has a certain allegiance to his agency as well as a commitment to his client, and does not believe that working for the best interests of each means he has mutually exclusive goals. Besides unearthing or developing needed community services or resources, the broker helps the client snip away at any red tape he encounters. In essence, the broker is more a participant than a spectator, and more facilitative than combative. He recognizes that to make a good referral, he must know what services exist, so he becomes a specialist in the resources available in his community. (Dancy 1972, P. 42)

As well as attention being given to the roles appropriate for paraprofessionals in general, it is to be expected that special consideration has been given to the use of indigenous mental health workers in particular. In one center in Harlingen, Texas, several of the staff professionals discussed the perceptions of the tasks and roles held by indigenous workers, which were formulated by the center's staff and advisory board members (Herbert, Chevalier, and Meyers 1974). In a report on the use of these workers, included were fourteen tasks indicated as being within the purview of indigenous workers. They are as follows:

- *Counseling:* providing contact, support, and guidance for mental patients, drug users, alcoholics, and their families through home and office visits.
- *Supervision of medication:* ensuring that the patient is taking the proper dosage and has an adequate supply of medication.
- *Follow-up:* contacting and working with patients after release from the state hospital or after referral by another agency or individual.
- *Transportation:* providing transportation for patients to the hospital in Harlingen, to the day center, to doctors appointments, and to other agencies.
- *Intake:* securing social histories, screening patients, and determining appropriate services.
- *Case staffing:* participating in intra-agency coordination, sharing information with and seeking information from other professional and nonprofessional staff, and making appointments for patients for medical and psychological evaluations.
- *Referral:* participating in the coordination of activities with other

social agencies and referring patients to welfare, vocational rehabilitation, or other agencies; attempting to locate jobs for patients.

- *Day-center work:* helping provide occupational, reactional, and group activities for patients.
- *Patient evaluation:* helping determine the patients' problems and develop a treatment plan.
- *Public education and information:* providing information to the public about services offered by the center and education about mental illness.
- *Community support:* recruiting volunteers and soliciting materials and other resources for the center.
- *Outreach:* locating unserved mentally ill persons (casefinding and encouraging referrals from individuals and agencies).
- *Recording:* completing administrative forms and daily case recording.
- *Inservice training:* participating in regular seminars with professionals concerning casework, interviewing methods, and particular case problems. (Herbert, Chevalier and Meyers 1974, Pp. 309-310)

Recruitment and Screening

Both the recruitment and initial evaluation of prospective mental health paraprofessionals have been very haphazard or ineffective processes in most instances. The reasons for this are varied:

1. Agencies have not been clear about the reasons underlying the employment of nonprofessionals, i.e. to alleviate unemployment, to involve persons who have overcome a specific problem such as alcoholism, to train psychologically aware paraprofessionals.

2. Community centers were unsophisticated in how to reach and motivate prospective applicants from the hard core unemployed.

3. There was a lack of awareness as to which were the most effective means of recruiting nonprofessionals—particularly indigenous personnel. Consequently, there was confusion and occasional conflict as to which of the following methods to employ: employment advertisements and agencies, community leaders (religious, business, etc.), handouts, posters, and or lectures to local groups.

4. Assessment procedures used in screening applicants were

often misdirected or inappropriate. Some were aimed at recruiting a certain type of individual that, as it turned out, was unacceptable to the community; in other instances, the person sought was not someone who would be creative and be a new source of talent, but one who could be easily transformed into a "pseudoprofessional."

The problems listed above, which were initially encountered by agency recruiters, have been dealt with to some degree now that the movement has gained some level of experience and hindsight. For example, it has been found that mass media is expensive and often not effective, whereas by posting notices and handing out circulars, one can reach many potential workers (Martin 1969; Schmais 1967).

The use of existing paraprofessionals is also beneficial. By having them pass the word regarding new openings, one can often recruit a high calibre of workers with the traits required by the agency. When nonprofessional mental health workers are included on screening and evaluation committees, the person chosen is often closer to the type seen as acceptable by the community, than when the board is made up exclusively of professionals. With this in mind, community mental health centers today now require that both professional and paraprofessional candidates be interviewed and approved by representatives of both prior to being accepted for employment.

Recruitment and assessment is still a difficult process at best. Agencies such as the Department of Health, Education, and Welfare have suggested a number of guidelines in hiring new paraprofessionals (see Fig. 4-1), but even in these instances, it has been difficult to put such guidelines into effect.

Key Attributes of Paraprofessionals*

• *An understanding of disadvantaged persons and communities.* Adequate understanding of the kind of persons and community to be served is regarded as essential. The concern is not with mere exposure to poverty but with genuine understanding of the special problems of living in poverty and of poor peoples' methods of adaptation to their circumstances. Typically, this is gained from living or working in a poverty area or from other work with the disadvantaged, such as at a Job Corps Center. Familiarity with poverty can be fairly readily determined by such indices as being on welfare roles, family income level, place of residence, and by self-reports on personal and family experience and on job and volunteer activities. However, this experience does not of itself ensure either an interest in helping other people or a depth of understanding. These must be explored through interviews and through reports of others who know the applicant well.

• *Ability to communicate with the persons to be served, to win their confidence, to help them, and above all, to influence them.* Genuine respect for, and commitment to, the persons to be served are heavily involved in this skill, though they are not sufficient in themselves to ensure the required leadership ability. Moreover, such sensitivity and regard are not uniformly expressed from person to person; in one case a gentle manner, in another a more forthright, even tough, approach will reflect concern and consideration. The critical factor is the ability to influence and guide the individuals served in a way that will accomplish program objectives. This skill is most clearly seen in a "picture" of the individual's interactions with other persons in his usual environment. Such information, of course, is best obtained from the reports of his peers and others in the community. It is especially relevant to the relationships and functions of the job. For example, the ability to lead and persuade others in activities which are generally socially disapproved may be a skill transferable to some human services support positions. Reports by social caseworkers on applicants in families on welfare (such reports to be made only with the applicant's permission) can be valuable in bringing occupational potential to light.

• *Adaptability, dependability and perseverance.* For individuals being hired in a merit career position, as contrasted with placement in a rehabilitation training project, reasonable ability to adapt and to develop responsible work habits is to be expected. This is doubly important for those human services support positions which entail assistance to others in establishing such personal discipline. Some assessment of an applicant's adaptability and responsibility can be made through self-report of activities on an application form or in an interview. Reports of others who have had the opportunity to observe the individual in paid or volunteer work, or in home responsibilities, are essential. Conventional employment and academic criteria are not necessarily pertinent, and arrest records (and even some types of convictions) should not be automatically disqualifying.

· *Ability to learn the technical aspects of the job, and potential for advancement with training.* This requirement varies greatly with the nature and level of the particular human services support position. Although technical skills without the essential human relations skills may well be worthless, most human services support functions require more than rapport with clients to succeed in accomplishing program objectives.

For jobs with the least complex technical requirements only an elementary level of reading and writing may be required. In some cases, such as preprofessional jobs in the Employment Service program, minimal literacy while necessary is not of primary importance. For certain other support positions, the ability to handle more complex written material, such as preparing simple reports and comprehending agency releases, may be needed. The pertinent level of ability to follow oral and written instructions may be assessed rather informally through the application materials and interview, or more carefully through oral directions and literacy tests, as appropriate. For many of the support classes these methods of assessment are most appropriately used only as a basis for qualifying. But whatever the method, even if it is nothing more than the applicant's ability to complete a simple application card on his own, it must be administered and evaluated on a consistent, standardized basis for all applicants.

For specific job-related technical skills and knowledge, evidence from instructors and supervisors about the applicant's performance in pertinent training and about his paid or volunteer experience is particularly desirable. Especially for some of the higher level support classes, performance, oral, or practical written tests covering required technical areas can be useful. Written tests which emphasize academic achievement are not appropriate.

The interview panel or selection board should give some attention to the applicant's potential to advance, with training, up the career ladder envisaged for the type of work. For this purpose, indices from past behavior must focus on evidences of growth more than on present level of skill or achievement. To the extent that advancement necessitates mastery of relatively formal training on or off the job, pertinent oral, performance, and written tests can be useful assessment devices. Motivation, not just for advancement but for undertaking the responsibilities that lead to advancement, is perhaps as critical as the ability to advance. In this connection, evidence of previous efforts in seeking employment, training, and other avenues for self-improvement would seem particularly pertinent.

Guidelines on Recruitment and Selection Methods for Support Classes in the Human Services. Office of State Merit Systems, Department of Health, Education, and Welfare, U.S. Government Printing Office, Washington, D.C., 1968, pp. 6–8.

Figure 4-1. Key attributes of paraprofessionals.

Training

Educational programs in mental health technology have grown in the past several years. In the late 1960's there were only a few, but now there are close to 200 undergraduate programs in the area.

Some of these programs are broad-based systems in the human services which have several course options directed toward specific positions in education, social work, or mental health technology (see Fig. 4-2). Others are specifically directed at future mental health technology workers.

FIRST YEAR

First Semester	Credits
361 English Composition I (3;0)	3
History I Elective (3;0) [530]	3
844 Introduction to Human Services (3;0)	3
810 Basic Psychology (3;0)	3
840 Introduction to Sociology (3;0)	3
Physical Education Elective (0;2)	1
	16

Second Semester	
362 English Composition II (3;0)	3
812 Psychology of Adjustment (3;0)	3
842 Social Problems (3;0)	3
History II Elective (3;0) [532]	3
846 Social Work Processes (3;0)	3
Physical Education Elective (0;2)	1
571 Critical Analysis and Problems in Health (1;0)	1
	17

SECOND YEAR

First Semester	
Social Science Electives (3;0) (3;0)	3 and 3
Psychology Elective (3;0)	3
848 Urban Community Development Field Work I (1;4) *or*	
Social Science Elective (3;0)	3
934 Introduction to Counseling and Guidance (3;0)	3
Mathematics Elective (3;0) [681 or 683]	3
	18

Second Semester	
849 Urban Community Development Field Work III (2;8)	6
Science Elective (3;0 or (2;4) [130 or 180]	3 or 4
Liberal Arts Elective (3;0)	3
787 Metropolitan Government (3;0)	3
	15 or 16

Figure 4-2. Human Services Curriculum, Case Aide Option, for Camden County College, Blackwood, New Jersey: Students are trained for paraprofessional positions in community service fields, including education, health, mental health, social services, recreation, and rehabilitation. Source: Camden County College *Bulletin* 1975–1976.

The latter type of program is often set up as an associate degree plan in mental health technology, with the provision that the person can continue on to pursue a bachelor's program if so desired. Such a curriculum usually involves a heavy emphasis on clinical courses and practice in field placements. Therefore, the program is usually longer than conventional ones in other areas.

The program at Hahnemann Medical College and Hospital's College of Allied Health Profession is ⅔ year long (see Fig. 4-3). It is set up to assist the student to explore both traditional and innovative models in the human services. Latitude and supervision is provided so that the student can apply the skills learned to the field placement in a personal manner.

Mental Health Associate Degree Program

The Hahnemann Department of Mental Health Sciences has recently developed an educational program, emphasizing the mental health field, at the Associate Degree Level.

This program is a 3 year program which leads to an Associate Degree in Mental Health Technology. The curriculum is designed to provide a sound foundation in basic liberal arts subjects, e.g. English, the Humanities and the Social Sciences, allowing the interested graduate to gain ready access into a Bachelors level college, and further career development. There is heavy emphasis on Psychology and Sociology courses to provide an underpinning in these two twin behavioral sciences.

In addition to the basic liberal arts coursework, a mental health seminar will be held throughout each of the three years over which the program will extend. The seminar will encourage the students to examine and characterize new roles in the mental health field in relation to the philosophy and practice of community mental health. The seminar will critically explore old and new models for human service delivery with particular reference to the mental health system. In the second and third year the seminars will be directly related to the field placements and will serve as a vehicle for discussion regarding case and community activities. Content of the seminar will encompass such areas as therapeutic modalities, community resources and outreach, interviewing principles, psychopharmacology, remotivation, rehabilitation and crisis intervention.

During the 2nd and 3rd year, the student will be assigned field placements at various mental health and human services centers within the city of Philadelphia.

The unique aspect of this program is that the student can continue to work while earning his/her degree. It can be seen as a first step in a "career ladder" which can lead to a Bachelor's Degree in Mental Health Technology and even graduate training. It is also anticipated that the training will give the student increased job mobility, as well as role flexibility in mental health settings.

MENTAL HEALTH ASSOCIATE
DEGREE PROGRAM

First Year

Eng.	101	Composition & Literature I	3
Eng.	102	Composition &	3
		Literature II	3
M.H.	101	Introduction to Psychology	3
M.H.	201	Abnormal Psychology I	3
M.H.	202	Abnormal Psychology II	3
Eng.	107	Communications	
M.H.	111	Clinical Practice Seminar I	2
M.H.	112	Clinical Practice Seminar II	2
M.H.	113	Clinical Practice Seminar III	2

Total Quarter Hours for First Year   24

Second Year

		Mathematics I	3
		Mathematics II	3
		Humanities Elective	3
		Humanities Elective	3
		Humanities Elective	3
P.S.	101	American National Government	3
M.H.	114	Clinical Practice Seminar I	2
M.H.	115	Clinical Practice Seminar II	2
M.H.	116	Clinical Practice Seminar III	2
M.H.	121	Clinical Training I	4
M.H.	122	Clinical Training II	4
M.H.	123	Clinical Training III	4

Total Quarter Hours for Second Year   36

Third Year

		Human Biology I	3
		Human Biology II	3
		Human Biology III	3
Soc.	105	Introduction to Sociology	3

Soc.	203	Social Psychology I	3
Soc.	204	Social Psychology II	3
M.H.	217	Clinical Practice Seminar I	2
M.H.	218	Clinical Practice Seminar II	2
M.H.	219	Clinical Practice Seminar III	2
M.H.	221	Clinical Training I	4
M.H.	222	Clinical Training II	4
M.H.	223	Clinical Training III	4
		Total Quarter Hours for Third Year	36
		Total Quarter Hours for Graduation	96

Figure 4-3. The College of Allied Health Professions' (Hahnemann Medical College and Hospital) mental health associate degree program.

The establishment of human services associate and bachelor's level programs was often quite a demanding task-particularly in traditional college settings. One requirement that gave institutions difficulty was the establishment of liaison with the community and institutional facilities in mental health where the field work would be done.

Another problem was recruiting faculty that was appropriate. Since this was a practical program, i.e. one that was to prepare the student for a position after graduation, it required a staff that was functioning in the field. Also, in the academic areas which were not in the technical major area (community mental health), the teachers had to be willing to help the student learn the material. If an English or math teacher was rigid and expected the student from a low-income, educationally deprived area to pick up the information as quickly as the student in the college from a high school which provided a good academic basis, many of the potential workers would never pass or graduate.

One of the positive factors to arise out of the development of the new mental health technology programs was the interaction it forced between professionals from the normally divided areas of psychology, social work, and psychiatry. Persons belonging to these separated professions (see Appendix 5 for the breakdown on these three areas) got an opportunity to see places of mutual interest and activity; thus, interdisciplinary efforts were indirectly furthered through their meeting and interaction within the programs.

Institutional Training

Pre-service and in-service training of nonprofessionals was also carried out by the community mental health agencies and hospitals themselves. In this way they could tailor the educational input to their own needs and the individual requirements of each student.

Hospitals and community centers usually have staff members who have a good deal of clinical experience and are used to providing in-service courses to new professionals and nonprofessionals, i.e. psychiatric aides, as well as students and interns in nursing, psychology, and allied areas. Courses which are relevant and based on the facility's current mode of operation can be provided then at the employing institution.

On-the-job training is also more easily coordinated within the institution if they are the ones conducting the entire educational program. There is no substitute for good supervised experience. Books and courses are helpful; field work is *irreplaceable*.

The problem in institutional programs is that in being specialized they sometimes become too narrow. While the institutional programs are practical, they often do not qualify for academic credit and thus stymie the educational advancement of the participant. So, after spending several months or years in the program, little academic credit is given it by institutions granting B.A./B.S. and advanced degrees when one of these people enters college.

Today, one way around this is the experience credits given by degree-granting institutions. However, often the applicant gets quite a bit less than is deserved.

Regarding the breadth of the program, institutional programs often suffer in this area as well. While they provide good technical training, they often ignore areas which help the person grow—professionally and personally. English courses help in better report writing and reading skills necessary for advancement and math skills are often needed if additional professional training is to be sought, but too often these areas are left out of hospital and community training programs that are unaffiliated with a college.

The solution seems to be to get local community colleges and universities affiliated with area health-providing agencies. This answer has in fact been viewed by man as appropriate and has been acted upon already in many states. However, even in such instances as these, the joining has been accomplished haphazardly, and the ties are thus tenuous, a better evaluation of college-community health programs is now required. If this is done, then the most suitable and continuously progressive and flexible programs can be developed: The result would be better for the clients and improved job status for the human services worker.

Figure 4-4. Psychologist training mental health workers in techniques of group counseling. (Photo courtesy of Hahnemann Medical College & Hospital, Philadelphia.)

Final Comments

The mental health paraprofessionals, be they indigenous or not, are currently having great impact on the delivery of human services both in the traditional institution, such as the hospital, and in the innovative satellite clinics of the community mental health center. Recruitment, screening, and training procedures are being improved, and career ladders are being established, but we are far from reaching what can be termed a "successful" goal in this area.

Professionals are still arguing within their own groups as well as between associations. How then can we expect them to join together and help formulate with the community the roles and areas of potential effectiveness of the new professionals in mental health? Some positive steps toward progress have been made through the interdisciplinary efforts made by some in the field. However, much still must be done. Despite the great progress that is yet to be made before we can truly see the full potential of the paraprofessional movement, one can not help but be optimistic. After all, look how far we have already come.

REFERENCES

Albee, G. A.: *Mental Health Manpower Trends: Manpower For Mental Health.* Kentucky Mental Health Manpower Commission, Louisville, 1969.

Arieti, Silvano and Lorraine, Sally: The therapeutic assistant in treating the psychotic. *International Journal Of Psychiatry, 10,* 11-22, 1972.

Dancy, Ricky: The broker: a new specialist for the community mental health center. *Hospital & Community Psychiatry, 23,* 221-23, 1974.

Herbert, George K., Chevalier, Marc C., and Meyers, Charles L.: Factors contributing to the successful use of indigenous mental health workers. *Hospital & Community Psychiatry, 25,* 308-10, 1974.

Martin, J. M.: Recruitment and community penetration. In *Breakthrough for Disadvantaged Youth.* U.S. Department of Labor, Manpower Administration, Washington, D.C., 1969.

McPheeters, Harold L., King, James B., and Teare, Robert J.: The middle-level mental health worker: I: His role. *Hospital & Community Psychiatry, 23*(11), 329-34, 1972.

Mosher, Lorene R., Reifman, Ann, and Menn, Alma. Characteristics of nonprofessionals serving as primary therapists for acute schizophrenics. *Hospital & Community Psychiatry, 24*(6), 391-96, 1973.

Robinson, G. Erlick and Alboim, Naomi: The use of non-professional change agents in an institution. *Canadian Psychiatric Association Journal, 19*(5), pp. 469-72.

Schmais, A.: *Implementing Nonprofessional Programs in the Human Services.* Center for the Study of Unemployed Youth, New York, 1967.

Shelley, Edward M. and Fieve, Ronald R.: The use of nonphysicians in a health maintenance program for affective disorders. *Hospital & Community Psychiatry, 25*(5), 303-5, 1974.

Sobey, Francine: *Non-Professional Personnel in Mental Health Programs.*

National Institute of Mental Health, U.S. Government Printing Office, Washington, D.C., 1969.

Spergel, S.: *Community Problem Solving: The Delinquency Example.* Univ. of Chicago Press, Chicago, 1969.

Chapter 5

VOLUNTEERS IN MENTAL HEALTH*

VOLUNTEERISM IN MANY FIELDS is merely an exercise in tokenism or superficiality. One, or several volunteers, may be used simply to demonstrate that nonsalaried personnel are in evidence. In other instances, the numbers of volunteers present may be high, but their activities are limited strictly to routine chores—even though their talents or experience would seem to dictate otherwise.

Despite the undeniable presence of some poorly structured volunteer programs, volunteerism in mental health has generally been sophisticated and extensive for a long period of time. Certain volunteer programs have developed a cadre of workers to supplement the existing roles of paid professionals and paraprofessionals. In other situations, volunteers have established self-help groups essentially on their own.

In both cases, community participation and leadership in providing organized mental health assistance to their neighbors have proved helpful and *necessary*. Without these efforts, many people affected with emotional problems or opiate, gambling, or alcohol habits might go unaided. Students, professionals, retired persons, nonprofessionals, clerics, and business executives have all contributed to the complex multilevel volunteer movement in mental health.

As in other fields, the process has not been without its problems, but neither has it been without its creative advances. It has produced key leaders and initiated positive interest in noted detractors. Yet, all in all, the movement is shown less for its spectacular positive and negative aspects as it is for the gradual, but continually progressive, impact it has had on the overall human services movement of the nation. It is because of this steady impact that this chapter has been included.

---

*See also Appendix 6.

COORDINATION OF VOLUNTEERS

Volunteerism fluorishes when it is well organized. One way of doing this is to establish a resource center for volunteer programs. One such center is the *Volunteer Action Council (VAC)* in Philadelphia.

The Volunteer Action Council, Inc. was formerly called the Council on Volunteers. It was organized under the auspices of the Community Chest of Philadelphia in 1946. It was organized to coordinate and direct the efficient use of volunteers during the post World War II period. In 1950, the Council on Volunteers (COV) became a department of the Health and Welfare Council, a regional planning and research agency of the United Fund of Philadelphia.

The major role of the COV in the 1940s and 1950s was interviewing and referring volunteers, the establishment of standards for volunteer services (see Fig. 5-1), and the development of the position of Director of Volunteers in agencies. In the 1960s, however, the Council's role expanded to include consultation, education, coordination, and promotion of new concepts in voluntarism.

Standards for Volunteers*

What do we mean by standards? Most agencies/organizations that utilize volunteers are interested in good volunteer programs, that certain principles are involved, and that good practice is essential. Standards are not just something to be put on paper but are meant to be applied. The following are key points to use as guidelines in the development of standards for volunteers.

1. The administration executive and Board of Directors lend support and backing to the program.
2. Provision has been made for a central volunteer office/department with adequate staff to administer it.
3. The staff is committed to volunteerism and see the volunteers as valuable coworkers.
4. The agency staff has good motivation. Volunteers are seen as a good public relations resource, making a good impression for the agency in the community. They also are seen as releasing time of the professional staff by covering clerical duties the professional staff would otherwise perform.
5. There are worthwhile jobs for volunteers to do, jobs created with the full cooperation of staff. Jobs are well-defined, and when a new volunteer job is being considered, it is thoroughly discussed with and approved by the staff.
6. Interviewing of volunteers is a procedure essential to the organization. Selecting the right persons for the right jobs, creating new volunteer opportunities based on individual skills and supplementing staff skills are all advantages derived from good interviewing procedures.
7. No volunteer is finally accepted who does not complete the agency training course, and what is more important, no volunteer is finally accepted until after try-out on the job under an agency's supervision and written approval and evaluation by the agency supervisor. Assignments, thus, can be made on the basis of careful selection and the fitting of each volunteer to the job he can best do.
8. Supervision is thoughtful and based on close contact with the volunteer. Refresher courses are given regularly and efforts are made to give volunteer opportunities for growth and increased responsibility.
9. Careful records are kept and follow-up is important.
10. The development and maintenance of an ongoing volunteer committee, written personnel policies relating to volunteer service, and yearly volunteer recognition events.

Figure 5-1.

*Source: Handout, Volunteer Action Council, Philadelphia.

In 1970, the National Center for Voluntary Action was established in Washington, D.C., and the Council played an active part in the development of this national program. The Philadelphia Council on Volunteers was one of the volunteer bureaus chosen to serve as a Voluntary Action Center in this pilot project. Now more than 250 Voluntary Action Centers are in operation throughout the United States.

Today, the Volunteer Action Council, Inc./Voluntary Action Center serves Philadelphia, Delaware, and Montgomery Counties of Pennsylvania. VAC is an independent, nonprofit agency of the United Fund of Philadelphia and an affiliate of the National Center for Voluntary Action and the Association of Volunteer Bureaus of America.

Figure 5-2. Volunteer helping in the rehabilitation of the handicapped. (Photo courtesy of Volunteer Action Council, Philadelphia.)

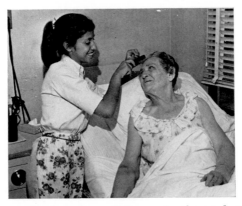

Figure 5-3. An ego brush-up is needed even by the aged, as given by one young student volunteer. (Photo courtesy of United Fund.)

Figure 5-4. An adult volunteer can be of great help as a friend and as an older model to emulate. (Photo courtesy of Friends Neighborhood Guild.)

Services Offered by VAC

VAC provides a wide range of services to individuals, citizen groups, business, and industry, as well as to the community at large.

To *individuals* VAC offers:

1. A wide variety of volunteer opportunities in agencies, organizations, and institutions in the tri-county area it serves.

2. Personal interviews and placement.

3. Centralized information and referral services.

4. Special projects and planned recruitment programs.

To *citizen groups, business, and industrial* VAC offers consultation services:

1. To aid in the development and operation of their own volunteer service programs.

2. To assist in planning education and training programs related to volunteer services.

3. To illustrate how corporate social responsibilities can be met through business involvement in voluntarism.

4. To help in the development of guidelines for volunteer placement services provided by employers for employees.

5. To offer group and corporate projects utilizing volunteers.

To the *community* the Volunteer Action Council offers:

1. Counsultation service to agencies and organizations for matters pertaining to the development and administration of volunteer programs.

2. Standards for volunteer service.

3. Assistance to agencies and organizations in the planning for orientation, training, and supervision of volunteers and volunteer administrators.

4. Educational programs to enhance the skills and abilities of volunteer administrators and volunteers.

5. Consultation service to agencies and organizations for matters concerning citizen participation on community boards.

6. Techniques for recognition of volunteers in community services.

7. Directories listing volunteer opportunities for adults and youth.

Figure 5-5. A new volunteer receives information from experienced volunteer coordinator. (Photo courtesy of Volunteer Action Council, Philadelphia.)

Figure 5-6. Volunteers waiting to sign up new youth workers.   (Photo courtesy of Volunteer Action Council, Philadelphia.)

Figure 5-7. New volunteer signing up to work with youth in the community. (Photo courtsey of Volunteer Action Council, Philadelphia.)

In general, the VAC serves both the individual and the community by conducting a public relations and community information program through publications, publicity, a volunteer resources library, and an active speakers bureau.

With the current acceptance of nonprofessionals as members of the treatment team and the need for some dislocated workers to gain new training via voluntarism in other fields, organizations such as the Volunteer Action Council have been as busy as ever, as can be seen in the increased demands they have been required to meet (see Fig. 5-8).

1974-75 PROGRAM REVIEW*

PROMOTION AND COORDINATION

Program planning during 1974-75 resulted in a number of major accomplishments. In April, 1975, VAC sponsored VOLUNTEER RECOGNITION WEEK honoring those volunteers who contributed more than three-quarters of a million service hours in the tri-county area. Seven individuals, three service agencies, and a major Philadelphia business received Volunteer-of-the-Year Awards.

Early in 1975 the National Federation of Business and Professional Women's Clubs of Japan visited VAC. The women were sponsored by the Japanese Ministry of Education; voluntary action was of particular interest to them. This cultural interchange resulted in a greater understanding of the world-wide impact of volunteerism.

Additional accomplishments in volunteer promotion included the establishment of a speaker's bureau, and the printing and distribution of 1500 directories listing adult and youth volunteer opportunities in the tri-county area.

The promotion of inter-agency cooperation was another program accomplishment. VAC's participation in the Philadelphia Festival furthered cooperation among three organizations; ACTION, The Greater Philadelphia Cultural Alliance and Delaware Valley Association-Directors of Volunteer Programs (DVA-DVP). This year VAC also established new organizational ties with the Southeastern Region, Volunteer Coordinators' Association (SERVCA). As a result of a management-program study, VAC received a full accreditation from the Association of Volunteer Bureaus in December, 1974.

EDUCATION AND TRAINING

Plans to establish a volunteer resource library at VAC began in 1975. This year VAC developed its clearinghouse services, and served as the liaison between the National Center for Voluntary Action's informational sources and local volunteer agency requests.

During 1974-75, VAC assisted volunteer directors in program planning, volunteer recruitment, training and orientation. The organization also aided in planning the Board Member's Institute and SERVCA and DVA-DVP's workshop programs.

INTERVIEWING AND REFERRAL

During 1974-75, VAC served as a referral point for individuals seeking volunteer opportunities and as a center for volunteer recruitment; distributed the Volunteer Opportunities directories; developed an interview and referral program; surveyed agency needs and the potential for placement of handicapped volunteers; and initiated plans for the efficient utilization of volunteers during the bicentennial.

These activities have resulted in the placement of more than three hundred eighty volunteers in various agencies and organizations in the tri-county area.

CONSULTATION

This year VAC provided ongoing consultation services pertaining to the development and administration of volunteer programs to seventy-eight different agencies and organizations. Health and welfare agencies, governmental agencies, hospitals, businesses, medical and cultural institutions, and citizen and professional groups worked with VAC to meet their program needs.

The specific consultation services to these agencies and organizations included administrative techniques; program planning and evaluation; volunteer recruitment; training and orientation; communication; and personnel practices and procedures relating to staff/ volunteer relationships.

Additionally, VAC served on the United Fund's Volunteer Committee and assisted in the preparation of the "United Fund Volunteer Handbook."

Figure 5-8.

However, despite the work of VAC and other coordination and resource centers, there are activities that such organizations do *not* perform. For example, VAC does *not* have its own pool of volunteers, provide campaign solicitors, or refer persons to paid work.

While they provide consultation, it is up to the individual

---

*Source, Volunteer Action Council, Inc., *Annual Report,* June 1, 1974–May 31, 1975.

agencies to develop *on-going* programs in recruiting, screening, training, and utilizing volunteers. While resource centers advise individual agencies and provide standards for volunteers (see Fig. 5-1), to see how volunteers function in today's society, one has to turn to the voluntary, i.e. crisis hotline, and self-help agencies that are involved in using them.

Figure 5-9. A young volunteer helping prepare food for children at a day care center. (Photo courtsey of United Fund.)

Figure 5-10. Buttons awaiting new volunteers. (Photo courtesy of Volunteer Action Council, Philadelphia.)

HOTLINES

Not too far back in the past, the idea of a crisis telephone service staffed by volunteers might have been considered quite a radical experiment. However, within the past decade, the so-called "hotline" has become a standard feature within most large cities.

Telephone Crisis Service in Nonmetropolitan Areas

The success of crisis telephone services in major urban centers has led much smaller communities to experiment with its use. One such operation in a nonmetropolitan area was initiated in Midland, Michigan, in 1970. This service was set up in a county with a population of only 65,000—a number far less than in the sprawling, heavily populated communities where a hotline is usually found (Greene and Mullen 1973).

Recruitment for this program progressed in the first year of operation from word of mouth to the point where a training course attracting an average of twenty-five people is now held for volunteers approximately every five months. The training in this setting involves not only lectures, but also role playing and small group discussion as well.

Audio tapes of previously recorded crisis calls are played to provide practical illustrations of what one might expect. Information is also presented in such areas as psychopathology, drug abuse, crisis intervention theory, and suicide prevention, to name only a few. Following the initial training, in-service sessions are held every two months.

The overall goal of the training is to assist the volunteer to be able to draw out callers and help them ventilate their feelings; relieving immediate pent-up pressures helps the caller to see alternatives and grasp the belief that there are other solutions. By encouraging verbalization, the volunteer can also see if the caller needs to be referred to a community resource. Such a resource might be one that was in a position to deal more extensively with drug/alcohol problems, family planning, legal aid, or psychotherapy.

One of the interesting facets of this nonmetropolitan program is the way calls are processed during the off-hours. (During the day they are handled by special trained secretaries.) In the large cities, volunteers are usually requested to maintain the phones in the hotline center. However, because of the low volume of night calls (averaging twenty per week) in a hotline agency servicing a smaller population, having people spend long hours in a center would be impractical.

Accordingly, in this program, incoming calls are received by an answering service and then patched into the volunteer who is at home. According to Doctors Robert Greene and Frank Mullen, this method of handling calls has some quite positive points. For example, they note "that when the telephone wakens the volunteer at, say, 3 AM, he hears a calm, factual message from the answering service rather than the anxiety and confusion of a person under stress. While returning the call, the volunteer has a few moments to collect his thoughts and provide a more effective response" (Greene and Mullen 1973, p. 95).

Another factor more peculiar to small nonmetropolitan hotline services than to ones covering a large area concerns the question of confidentiality. The chances of the volunteer knowing the caller is naturally increased in small populations. To handle this, the Midland program provided special training on the importance of maintaining confidentiality.

They emphasized not talking about the calls outside of the hotline center. Also, if the volunteer knew the caller, the volunteer was told to discuss with the caller whether this would interfere with their working together on the phone to solve the problem in which case another volunteer could be assigned to help. Other more extensive methods were also employed to increase the level of confidentiality (Greene and Mullen 1973). The total result was that the hotline volunteers were strongly impressed with the value of confidentiality to the success of their overall efforts.

"HELLO, THIS IS CONTACT! MAY I HELP YOU?"

These are the first words the lonely, the sick, the frightened hear when they telephone CONTACT PHILADELPHIA.

WHAT IS CONTACT?

It is a 24 hour crisis intervention telephone service staffed by caring and accepting volunteers who have received 50 hours of special training. It is an opportunity for YOU to reach out to the lonely, the sick at heart, the burdened, those who are desperate for help.

CONTACT traces its beginning to the enormously successful Life Line movement that originated in the Central Methodist Church of Sydney, Australia, in 1963, and which has grown to more than 100 cities around the world.

Participation in CONTACT means *dedication*. *Dedication* of your time for training as well as your effort to help keep the program going 24 hours a day, 7 days a week. Qualified workers, backed by professional volunteers, will serve eight hours per month at the telephone room. *Dedication* to the belief that people need your empathetic listening. The 50 hours of training will help you gain inner strength and insights to reach out to someone who needs to hear your warm, friendly, unshockable voice. As required by CONTACT National Headquarters at Harrisburg, Pennsylvania, you will have professional instruction and reality practice from lecturers in mental health, the social services and the religious community. We do not become psychologists or advice columnists. We do not judge or condemn. Instead, we learn the techniques that help people to seek their own solutions from their own inner resources. Each trainee will be evaluated for maturity and motivation.

In addition to handling approximately 3000 calls per month, CONTACT provides two other services—Reassurance calls for shut-ins and a teletype message service for the deaf.

Our membership is drawn from the total community in terms of age level, occupation, race, faith, and socioeconomic level.

Will you join us? Please do! But return the enclosed application promptly as classes are limited in size.

Figure 5-11. Excerpt from a CONTACT recruitment leaflet explaining how their crisis hotline in Philadelphia works.

Contact: An Urban Hotline Service

Contact is the name for an interfaith, interracial, nonprofit, twenty-four-hour-a-day telephone service in Philadelphia. It is a good illustration of a hotline service being operated by volunteers in an urban setting.

Contact is part of Life Line International which was formed on March 16, 1963 in Sydney, Australia. This international organization which accredited Contact and was the model for it, was begun by Doctor Alan Walker, pastor of the Central Mission in Sydney, because of a belief he had that much good would come from founding a telephone ministry.

Doctor Walker believed he could reach many of the "unreachables" by telephone who could not be contacted through his personal ministry in the church. When a woman in his parish district committed suicide, and he read subsequently in her diary her brief lonely entries—all of which ended with the phrase, "Nobody came"—he felt that someone must begin to reach out to the lonely. He couldn't go back and save this woman who felt so alone that she imposed self-starvation to the point of death; however, he could establish a telephone life line that could be available to others in need.

With the founding of a telephone service, Doctor Walker recruited volunteers and trained them in listening methods and basic principles in mental health. His work was the model for Contact and services like it.

Contact itself was first conceived in late 1971 after a suicide of one the church members in a parish in Philadelphia. Its first class was formed in January, 1972. Fifty hours of training was provided by volunteer professionals within a twenty-five week span. Sixty-three people were graduated from the course; a second class followed it six months later. As well as the initial training offered, as in the pattern of most crisis telephone services, inservice training is also conducted on an ongoing basis.

Hotlines are not without their problems. The difficulties they experience are usually tied to problems within the individual volunteers. These problems may be of a technical nature. The volunteer may not know how to deal with a chronic caller who is continually abusive. Or, the difficulty can be within the personality of the volunteer. An example of this would be a caller who does not receive support, but is dictated to by an authoritarian hotline worker. Generally, however, these problems can be ironed out through good training and continual screening of the type of work volunteers do. Rather than creating greater problems, the hotline serves the beneficial function of letting one human being link up with another when loneliness becomes too great and other resources seem nonexistent.

SELF-HELP ORGANIZATIONS

Self-help groups have played an essential role in providing human services for many years. While the work they do is not new, they are still important today for the impact that they have even now in contemporary society.

These groups are founded on what is perceived to be a common problem among those who are initiating them. At first, the group tends to be made up of people who have successfully dealt with the problem which the group will focus on in an active, peer-related fashion. Usually they require personal commitment and involvement on the part of those requesting help. Responsibility is expected of each member for his/her own actions, but group support and frequent communication between members is usually present. Though each self-help group obviously is unique in its focus and particular approach, they have similar theoretical bases and methods of operation in many instances (Katz 1970).

To appreciate how such self-help groups function, we shall look at two of them: *Alcoholics Anonymous* and *Recovery, Inc.* Though there are many more of these self-help organizations, these two have shown themselves to be extremely effective and, thus, worthy of brief examination here.

Alcoholics Anonymous*

Alcoholics Anonymous is a worldwide fellowship of men and women who help each other to stay sober. They offer the same

*Section on Alcoholics Anonymous is excerpted with minor modification from *A Brief Guide to Alcoholics Anonymous* and *Twelve Steps and Twelve Traditions;* both publications are copyrighted by Alcoholics Anonymous World Services, Inc. and are reprinted here with their permission.

help to anyone who has a drinking problem and wants to do something about it. Since they are all alcoholics themselves, they have a special understanding of each other. They know what the illness feels like, and they have learned how to recover from it in A.A.

An A.A. member says, "I *am* an alcoholic"—even when he has not had a drink for many years. He does not say that he is "cured." Once a person has lost the ability to control his drinking, this A.A. member would explain, he can never manage to drink safely—or, in other words, he can never become "a *former* alcoholic" or " an *ex*-alcoholic." In A.A. he *can* become a sober alcoholic, a *recovered* alcoholic.

How Does A.A. Help the Alcoholic?

Through the example and friendship of the recovered alcoholics in A.A., the new member is encouraged to stay away from a drink "one day at a time," as they do. Instead of "swearing off forever" or worrying about whether he will be sober tomorrow, the alcoholic concentrates on not drinking right now—today.

By keeping alcohol out of his system, A.A. believes the newcomer takes care of only one part of his illness in that it gives his body a chance to get well. They also point to another part: If he is going to *stay* sober, he needs a healthy mind and healthy emotions, too. A.A. believes he should straighten out his confused thinking and unhappy feelings by following A.A.'s "Twelve Steps" to recovery. These steps *suggest* ideas and actions that the members believe can guide him toward a happy and useful life (see Fig. 5-12). In order to be in touch with other members and to learn about the recovery program, the new member goes to A.A. meetings regularly.

Twelve Steps of Alcoholics Anonymous*

---

1. We admitted we were powerless over alcohol—that our lives had become unmanageable.
2. Came to believe that a Power greater than ourselves could restore us to sanity.

3. Made a decision to turn our will and our lives over to the care of God *as we understood Him.*

4. Made a searching and fearless moral inventory of ourselves.

5. Admitted to God, to ourselves, and to another human being the exact nature of our wrongs.

6. Were entirely ready to have God remove all these defects of character.

7. Humbly asked Him to remove our shortcomings.

8. Made a list of all persons we had harmed, and became willing to make amends to them all.

9. Made direct amends to such people whenever possible, except when to do so would injure them or others.

10. Continued to take personal inventory, and when we were wrong, promptly admitted it.

11. Sought through prayer and meditation to improve our conscious contact with God, *as we understood Him,* praying only for knowledge of His will for us and the power to carry that out.

12. Having had a spiritual awakening as the result of these steps, we tried to carry this message to alcoholics and to practice these principles in all our affairs.

---

*Reprinted by permission A.A. World Services. Inc.

Figure 5-12.

What Are A.A. Meetings?

Alcoholics Anonymous is made up of almost 28,000 local groups in ninety-two countries. The people in each group get together, usually once or twice a week, to hold A.A. meetings of two main types:

1. At "open meetings," speakers tell how they drank, how they discovered A.A., and how its program has helped them. Members may bring relatives or friends, and usually anyone interested in A.A. is also welcome to attend "open meetings."

2. "Closed meetings" are for alcoholics only. These are group discussions, and any member who wants to may speak up, to ask questions, and to share his thoughts with his fellow members. At "closed meetings," each A.A. can get help with his personal prob-

lems with staying sober and with everyday living. Some other
A.A. will have had the same problems and can explain how he
handled them—often by using one or more of the Twelve Steps.

Who Runs A.A.?

A.A. has no real government. Each group is free to work out
its own customs and ways of holding meetings, as long as it does
not hurt other groups or A.A. as a whole. The members elect a
chairman, a secretary, and other group officers. These officers do
not give orders to anybody; mostly, their job is to see that the
meetings run smoothly. In the average group, new officers are
elected twice a year.

However, the individual group is not cut off from the rest of
A.A. Just as A.A. members help each other, so do A.A. groups.
Here are three of the means they use to exchange help:

1. Groups in the same area set up a central office or "intergroup" office.

2. Groups everywhere share their experiences by writing to
the A.A. General Service Office in New York City.

3. Groups in the U.S. and Canada choose representatives to
go to the A.A. General Service Conference, held once a year.

All these A.A. offices and the representatives at the conference
make *suggestions,* based on the experiences of many different A.A.
groups, but they do not make rules or issue commands to any
groups or members.

What Does A.A. NOT Do?

1. A.A. does *not* run membership drives to try to argue alcoholics into joining. A.A. is for alcoholics who *want* to get
sober.

2. A.A. does *not* check up on its members to see that they
do not drink. It helps alcoholics to help *themselves.*

3. A.A. is not a religious organization. Each member is free
to decide on his own personal ideas about the meaning of life.

4. A.A. is *not* a medical organization, and it does *not* give out
medicines or psychiatric advice.

5. A.A. does *not* run any hospitals, wards, or sanitariums or provide nursing services.

6. A.A. is *not connected* with any other organization, but A.A. does cooperate with organizations that fight alcoholism. Some members work for such organizations, but on their own —*not* as representatives of A.A.

7. A.A. does *not* accept money from sources outside A.A., either private or government.

8. A.A. does *not* offer any social services, does *not* provide housing, food, clothing, jobs, or money. It helps the alcoholic stay sober so he can earn these things for himself.

9. Alcoholics Anonymous lives up to the "Anonymous" part of its title. It does *not* want members' names to be told on TV or radio or in newspapers, and members do not tell other members' names to people outside A.A. Members are *not* ashamed of belonging to A.A.; they just want to encourage more alcoholics to come to A.A. for help. They do *not* want to make heroes and heroines of themselves simply for taking care of their own health.

Recovery, Inc.

Another noted self-help group is Recovery, Inc. It is a nonprofit organization which offers a self-help approach to prevent chronicity in nervous patients and relapses in former mental patients.

Recovery, Inc. was founded in 1937 by a small group of patients of the late Abraham A. Low, M.D.; the self-help method employed is based on Low's writings in his book *Mental Health Through Will Training*. The self-help group therapy employed is similar in orientation to types used by other groups formed by nonprofessionals to deal with a certain type of problem (see Fig. 5-13).

Comparison of Orthodox Psychotherapy & Self-Help Therapy*

APPROXIMATE COMPARISONS

Orthodox psychotherapy	*Self-help group therapy*
1. Professional, authoritative therapist.	Non-professional leaders, group parity.
2. Fee.	Free.
3. Appointments & records.	None.
4. Therapy-oriented milieu (psychiatrist's office, clinic, etc.).	Non-therapy oriented milieu (church rooms, community centers, etc.).
5. No family confrontation.	Family encouraged.
6. Psychiatrist is presumed normal, does not identify with patient.	Peers are similarly afflicted, identify with each other.
7. Therapist is not a role model, does not set personal examples.	Peers are role models, must set examples for each other.
8. Therapist is non-critical, non-judgmental, neutral, listens.	Peers are active, judgmental, supportive, critical talk.
9. Patients unilaterally divulge to therapist, disclosures are secret.	Peers divulge to each other, disclosures are shared.
10. Patients expect only to *receive* support.	Patients must also *give* support.
11. Concerned about symptom substitution if underlying causes are not removed.	Urges appropriate behavior, not concerned about symptom substitution.
12. Accepts disruptive behavior and sick role, absolves patient, blames cause.	Rejects disruptive behavior and sick role, holds member responsible.
13. Therapist does not aim to reach patient at "gut level."	Peers aim to reach each other at "gut level."
14. Emphasis on etiology, insight.	Emphasis on faith, will-power, self-control.
15. Patient's improvement is randomly achieved.	Patient's behavior is planfully achieved.
16. Therapist-patient relationship has little direct community impact.	Peers' intersocial involvement has considerable community impact.

17. Everyday problems subordinated to long-range cure.	Primary emphasis on day-to-day victories: another day without liquor or drugs, another day without panic, etc.
18. Extra curricular contact and socialization with psychiatrist discouraged.	Continuing support and socialization available.
19. Lower cumulative drop-out percentage.	Higher drop-out percentage.
20. Patient cannot achieve parity with psychiatrist.	Members may themselves become active therapist.

Figure 5-13.

Recovery is not set up to replace the psychologist, psychiatrist, physician, or other professional. It does not offer diagnostic or counseling services, as such. Instead, it is a service for self-motivated adults.

Recovery training includes the practice of Doctor Low's techniques, regular attendance at meetings and study of the literature on the approach. Group meetings are held weekly and are conducted by members experienced in the approach; all of them were once people seeking help because of emotional problems. During the meetings, which usually last for about two hours, members give examples of specific difficulties they have had and how they used the Recovery method to deal with them.

As in other self-help groups, the treatment in Recovery, Inc. does not attempt to conduct deep analysis of problems, but instead discusses practical solutions to the problem of handling one's overt symptoms. When a new member presents problems, instead of being given an intellectual evaluation of them, he is presented with the reassuring response by other members in the group that they have experienced similar episodes themselves. Following this, other Recovery members note how they began to cope with such difficulties. The purpose of such discussions is to make the

*Source, From address by Dr. Stanley R. Dean delivered before the World Mental Health Assembly meeting in Washington, D.C., Nov. 18, 1969, included in the Congressional Record, *115* (191), Nov. 19, 1969.

new member feel he is not alone and that there is hope.

Many articles and papers have been written about Recovery, Inc. and other self-help groups (Roche 1975; Psychiatric News 1972; Crane 1968 provide a brief popular introduction). Though some negative points have been brought to the fore about them, i.e. group membership is merely a substitute for one's attachment to some other crutch such as symptoms, drugs, etc., one cannot ignore their positive results. Indeed, now after decades of ignoring such groups and their impressive effects, further study of them is in order to see what important aspects can be gained from them which can be applied to other areas in the human services.

MENTAL HEALTH ASSOCIATIONS

As well as the mental health-oriented self-help groups and voluntary action councils, the mental health associations of the United States have also served to increase the impact of voluntarism in the U.S. The dimensions of their programs are often extremely far reaching.

The following is an example of how one mental health association functions to serve the area of southeastern Pennsylvania:

The *Mental Health Association of Southeastern Pennsylvania* is an independent, nongovernmental, nonprofessional organization exclusively concerned with the mentally ill persons of their area. While the Association does not treat patients, it assesses needs, determines possible ways of meeting needs, and then tries to assure that those needs are met. The Association is a citizen's organization, which includes both laypersons and professionals in mental health, who aid the association in their spare time. The Association is supported by the United Fund, membership dues, and other sources, in lieu of being financed by taxes.

The five major program areas of the Association are as follows:

1. Comprehensive Community Services concerned with establishment and improvement of services and facilities for the prevention and treatment of mental illness.

2. Education Services, focusing on education and training related to mental health and mental illness.

3. Member Services, involved with recruitment, enrollment,

program dimensions...

Comprehensive Community Services involve all direct treatment facilities, including public mental hospitals, community mental health centers, clinics, mental health programs in general hospitals, private institutions, and all such agencies. The Association works for establishment and improvement of such services and facilities for the prevention and treatment of emotional illnesses.

Children and Adolescents are singled out here because special attention must be given this neglected group. Needs include accurate diagnoses, adequate treatment services, educational opportunities, coordination among community agencies, increased budgets as indicated, long-range planning for emotionally handicapped children, prevention, and research.

Education Services focus on training and education related to mental health and illness. These include cooperative ventures with consultation and education services of community mental health centers, schools, religious organizations, community groups and other health and welfare agencies. Training programs also are conducted for various groups of laymen and professionals who are not mental health specialists. An arm of Education Services is the Association's Parent Education and Human Relations Center which conducts full-scale programs for a variety of "common interest" groups.

Government Relations takes a key position in our current efforts, with other program areas tying in closely. Expansion is under way of liaison and service to appointed and government officials at federal, state, county, and community levels via a growing legislative network of area residents. Thanks to special consideration by United Fund, enabling employment of a Government Relations Director for the first time in July 1974, the Association is keeping better informed of pertinent government matters. In turn, our ability to inform officials of facts, needs, and progress in the mental health field also has improved. Growth in social action by the Mental Health Association is striking in this program area.

Member Services recruit and enroll citizen manpower for social action, financial support, and for program participation. "Number strength" is developed to help the Association carry out its goals. Members receive the Association's quarterly publication, "Lines of Communication". They are invited to all Association events in addition to special programs for members and are notified of important mental health matters.

Public Relations reflect Association goals, purposes, and activities in an effort to communicate effectively with individuals, groups, and the community at large. Public relations considerations are an integral part of all Association activity. Information about the Association and the mental health field is disseminated via mass media and printed publications prepared by the organization. Assistance is provided for mental health agencies having no public relations service of their own.

Figure 5-14a.

1976
1975
1974
1973
1966
1965
1963
1962
1961
1959
1956
1955
1953
1951

CAST FROM
SHACKLES
WHICH BOUND THEM
THIS BELL
SHALL RING OUT
HOPE FOR THE
MENTALLY ILL
AND VICTORY
OVER MENTAL ILLNESS

mental health association

Fear and despair, pain and suffering, may be the only companions of a mentally ill person. Surrounded by people, the mentally ill person may be alone. Often he truly cannot speak for himself. When he can, few listen. He is stripped of dignity and rights. Yet he is a citizen. A fellow citizen.

And the Mental Health Association of Southeastern Pennsylvania is a citizens' organization. It is made up of citizens who lend their support and voices to those who cannot speak for themselves. Citizens who take social action toward improved care and treatment, as well as prevention, of mental illnesses.

The Association was founded in 1951. It covers Chester, Delaware, Montgomery, and Philadelphia Counties and is an affiliate of Pennsylvania Mental Health, Inc., and the National Association for Mental Health.

Financial support comes from United Funds of Greater Philadelphia and Southeast Delaware County. We are dependent, too, upon membership contributions set at a minimum of $10 per person and $15 per family or other group.

The Association also receives grants from various foundations for special projects. These funds usually are not used for operating expenses but for projects outside the Association, such as hospitals, mental health centers, or schools. An exception is the recently opened Parent Education and Human Relations Center, an outgrowth of the Mental Health Association's long-established parent education program.

Active membership is needed to do the Mental Health Association's job. Members, joining forces with other concerned citizens, help the Mental Health Association to do the following:

- Improve laws affecting mentally ill persons of all ages
- Implement laws effectively for beneficial results
- Upgrade patient care for all age and diagnostic groups
- Support treatment and civil rights of all
- Reduce stigma hindering progress in the mental health field
- Fill gaps and lacks in mental health programs
- Conduct demonstration projects
- Strengthen our voice on behalf of mentally ill persons
- Finance the Association's important endeavors
- Meet current needs in the mental health field
- Plan the future through updated assessment of needs

Figure 5-14b.

and activities for members and potential members.

4. Government Relations, focusing on liaison and service to appointed and elected government officials at the federal, state, county, and community levels.

5. Public Relations, designed to develop and maintain a positive image with individuals, groups, and the community at large.

Final Comments on Voluntarism Today

Volunteers have frequently been depicted in a number of derogatory, simplistic ways. They have been viewed as "harmless or misinformed do-gooders" and as menial workers who can help only in the capacity of "juice distributors" and "card filers." Natuarally, this is far from the truth. Their work is often sophisticated and technical, but even when it is quite basic, the assistance it provides for both the agency and the volunteer can be quite remarkable.

As Harriet Naylor (1971), Director of Volunteer Services, State Department of Mental Hygiene, New York, correctly notes:

> Volunteer work helps most volunteers as much as it enriches the services to which they give their time and effort. In volunteering, people discover skills and capacities they did not know they had. The right to volunteer, to be on the given end, should be extended to all, and not be a privilege only for the "advantaged." It should enable people to work together with others quite different from themselves and thus discover commonality. (P. 26)

The roles volunteers play today are extremely varied and fit under the categories of direct service (counseling), administration, fund raising, and advocacy roles (being in the forefront of prison reform). In addition, they provide opportunities for young teenagers and senior citizens to contribute and learn in volunteer roles, at a time in their lives when salaried positions in new, challenging areas might not be open to them.

Volunteer opportunities for the young can open new worlds for them. They can see what areas they might be interested in, particularly in the human services fields, which are usually set up to effectively utilize their services.

Volunteer services can give people a chance to find themselves. As well as showing whether they would be interested in a certain position, interesting, nonsalaried positions can bring out the potential in people; volunteering can help decide which fields are *not* for them, as well as bring out potentials not realized before.

Volunteers are important, too. They can be behind training programs and social action projects that will have great impact on current public policy. They can receive training that will enable them to move into key positions that are salaried.

Today, voluntarism is not an exploitation of free labor, as it does not mean exercises in meaningless activity. Volunteer activities now are exercises in human growth for both the volunteer and the population the volunteer serves.

Volunteers fail only when the associations who serve as their conduit to important roles are lacking. Similarly, volunteers cease to be resources when the creativity among people is stymied by people/organizations who have failed to finally appreciate that volunteers are no longer equated with "do-gooders" and the "uninspired."

REFERENCES

Crane, Phil: Self-help in emotional illness. *Ligourian,* December 1968, pp. 100-102.

Greene, Robert J. and Mullen, Frank G.: A crisis telephone service in a nonmetropolitan area. *Hospital & Community Psychiatry, 24*(2), February 1973, pp. 94-97.

Katz, Alfred H.: Self-help organizations and volunteer participation in social welfare. *Social Work, 15,* January 1970, pp. 51-60.

Naylor, Harriet: New trends in volunteer services for the mentally handicapped. *Hospital & Community Psychiatry, 22*(4), April 1971, pp. 24-27.

Roche Reports: *Frontiers of Psychiatry, 5*(16), October 1975.

Study indicates "Recovery" doing well as self-help program. *Psychiatric News, 7*(14), July 19, 1972, p. 1.

PART III

THE HUMAN SERVICES MOVEMENT: A BROADER PICTURE

NEW CAREERS AND ASSOCIATE PROFESSIONALS IN
LAW ENFORCEMENT, COURTS, CORRECTIONS,
EDUCATION, SOCIAL WORK, AND MEDICINE

Chapter 6

POLICE

THE PARAPROFESSIONAL MOVEMENT in police work is bidirectional. Primarily it centers around the civilianization of formerly designated police controlled functions and the development of community service officer (CSO) programs. Additionally, the movement involves the training of police to fill roles normally reserved for professionals in the mental health and legal fields.

WHY CIVILIANIZATION?

Gerald Caplan (1975) of the National Institute of Law Enforcement succinctly points to the core reason for the use of paraprofessionals in police work: "The use of civilians in jobs traditionally performed by police officers has increased in recent years as police departments have sought to reduce costs and put more officers on the beat" (p. vi). However, cutting costs and improving personnel utilization are not the sole reasons for using a new cadre of nonuniformed staff members.

Other reasons for programs aimed at increasing the use of civilian volunteers and salaried workers in previously designated police roles include—

1. Attraction and involvement of youth in police work.
2. Enhancement of citizen involvement.
3. Improvement of social services and community relations functions of police departments.
4. Facilitation of minority group participation in law enforcement agencies.

While these and other motivating factors are intertwined with the two key reasons (money savings and optimal utilization of existing police personnel), they do merit separate attention since they have broadened the base of the paraprofessional movement in the law enforcement sector of criminal justice.

Cost Reduction

In police work, as in every other field contained under the human services umbrella, a prime reason for the use of paraprofessionals is due to the savings their employment produces. Utilization of civilians in place of uniformed personnel can be substantial.

W. C. Nemetz (1973), Chief of Police in Scottsdale, Arizona, indicates that his department "achieves substantial savings by maintaining close to a 30 percent ratio of civilian personnel to sworn officers . . . " (p. 20). His department calculated a salary savings of $13,000 when they conserved 6,000 officer-hours through the use of only four pre-college assistants (see Fig. 6-1).

Police Assistant
(Promotional)

Salary: $611–$780

Duties: This position will involve the responsibility for investigating motor vehicle accidents, writing routine police reports, such as burglary, misdemeanors, missing persons, stolen automobiles, preparing and delivering safety presentations to civic groups and related tasks.

Education: Graduation from a standard high school or completion of GED.

Necessary Special Requirements: Minimum Age—18 years. Minimum Height—5'8" (weight in proportion). Must possess a valid Arizona Motor Vehicle Operator's License. Must have sufficient correctable vision to adequately perform assigned duties.

Examination: To to announced.

Filing Date: Applications should be in the Personnel Office no later than 5:00 p.m., May 25, 1971.

Applications and further information may be obtained from the Personnel Office, City Hall, 3939 Civil Center Plaza, Scottsdale, Arizona.

* * *

Distinguishing Features of Work: This is general duty police work in the performance of tasks that do not necessarily require the expertise of a sworn officer.

The police assistant must possess the aptitude, integrity, and stability to perform parapolice functions, but maintain sufficient restraint not to become involved in matters requiring a sworn police officer.

Work is performed in accordance with departmental rules and regulations and police assistants receive assignments and instructions from police officers of higher rank. Work normally consists of report taking, preliminary investigation of certain criminal matters, accident investigation, and traffic regulation. Employees must be able to act without direct supervision and exercise independent judgment in meeting emergencies. Work methods and results are checked by superior officers through personal inspections, review of reports and discussions.

Examples of Work Performed: Any one position may not include all of the duties listed, nor do the listed examples include all of the tasks which may be found in positions of this class.

Investigates reports of bicycle theft, stolen autos, malicious mischief, missing persons, routine type burglary calls, frauds and embezzlements, thefts, delayed assault cases, motor vehicle accidents.

The police assistant will also handle calls relating to found property, bicycle impounds. He will also be responsible for the serving of summonses and subpeonas, the giving of safety talks in schools, before PTA and other civic groups, giving tours of the police building and any other assignments as the on-duty watch commander may deem necessary.

Required Knowledge, Skills and Abilities: Emphasis shall be placed on applicant's writing ability; especially in regard to grammar, clarity of thought, meaning and accuracy.

Ability to remember names, faces and details of accidents.

Ability to understand and carry out oral and written instructions.

Ability to deal courteously, but firmly, with the general public.

Ability to analyze situations and to adopt quick, effective and reasonable courses of action with due regard to surrounding hazards and circumstances.

Ability to prepare clear and comprehensive reports.

Education: Graduation from a standard high school or **GED**. Registered at, or planning to register at, one of the community colleges or Arizona State University.

Figure 6-1. Promotional advertisement for police assistant for Scottsdale, Arizona, Police Department.

Schwartz, Vaughn, Waller, and Wholey (1975) support these findings. They report that salaries average 23 percent less for civilians than for uniformed personnel. The overall savings of a civilian replacement program in terms of training and other "start-up" costs (equipment, etc.) are indicated by them to be an astonishing 96 percent.

Such savings are qualified though when one considers some of the problems which arise when police are replaced by civilians. They include (Schwartz et al. 1975) the following:

1. Increased complaints and lower morale among civilian because of divergence in training and pay between them and the uniformed force.

2. Higher attrition rate among civilians.

3. Police concern about the results of the policy of utilizing (possibly less reliable) civilians in the place of uniformed workers.

4. Higher incidence of absences and tardiness.

5. Lack of understanding of police role and/or job function resulting in less productive actions and a need for greater supervision.

Improved Personnel Utilization

Tied directly to the cost reduction offered by using civilians is the savings in terms of uniformed police personnel-work hours. Understaffing is often an issue in most law enforcement agencies. Particularly today, municipal and state budget cuts are forcing departments to curb hiring and even enforce lay-offs. Therefore, special efforts must be taken to increase police service in their essential crime prevention roles—especially in high crime areas (Trebach and Idelson 1970).

The desire to eliminate routine tasks which could be readily performed by others was the prime reason for the Fremont, California, Police Department study (Social Development Corporation 1973). This study sought to examine current police functions in order to determine how appropriate changes might be made in police curricula and job structure. Several products of this study were the initiation of several nonsworn police service technician positions, creation of a career ladder for them, and a reported enhancement of the police officer's position through reassignment of routine responsibilities to civilian officers.

Chief Nemetz (1973) of Scottsdale's police department (P.D.) agrees with the Freemont P.D.'s positive findings. While enthusiastic about the salary savings of civilian utilization, he says, "Perhaps more important, we have released patrolmen from the onerous and endless detail duty of routine investigations and reports— some 2,700 of them—and zeroed in on the work they like best and are trained to do: crime busting. It may be a coincidence, but it nevertheless is a fact that the incidence of major crimes in Scottsdale has dropped 9.8 percent during this period. Arrests have risen by 26.6 percent; citations increased by 17.8 percent and the morals of the force has risen accordingly" (p. 29).

VOLUNTEERS, PARAPROFESSIONALS, AND RECRUITMENT OF THE YOUNG

Involving young people in actual police work is yet another aspect of the paraprofessional movement in the law enforcement field. At the very least, such a procedure can serve to close the communication gap between the police and a segment of the youthful population.

In one such police-youth program (Goode 1970) male young adults (sixteen to twenty-one years of age) were selected to participate with regular officers to work on drives to stop automobile thefts and to prevent burglaries. Unlike many small projects, this pilot program in Jacksonville, Florida, listed 281 volunteer police youth patrolmen on the departmental roles in 1969. Considering the modest beginnings of the program just several months prior, one can speculate on the popularity of such a project.

> On Sunday, June 22, 1969, the first six Police Youth Patrolmen began riding as follows: one in Traffic; one in the Selective Enforcement Unit; three in Patrol; and one with the Police Community Relations Unit. This numerical riding division, eliminating Friday and Saturday nights from the riding schedule, was maintained in the Pilot Program. Also, in the Pilot Program, the Police Youth Patrolmen rode the evening watch only during the hours of 7 pm to 10:30 pm. The Police Youth Patrolmen reported to the assembly room

at Police Headquarters thirty minutes prior to their ride. These young men are taught to use the radio, how to read the daily patrol sheet, but in our eyes the most important training is the moral training.

For the first thirty days of the program, a member of the Police Community Relations Unit met with the officers and the Police Youth Patrolmen prior to their leaving the station to answer questions and hear suggestions for improvement of the program. The Police Community Relations Unit then rode the street for the remainder of the evening watch to be available in case of emergency. (Goode 1970, pp. 35-36)

While a thorough evaluation of this Jacksonville, Florida, experiment lacks a report of conclusive findings, it at least reflects a concrete effort on the part of one department to reduce miscommunication between the local youth and the police. Possibly an implicit mark of its success in the eyes of the officials in the Jacksonville P.D. was the establishment of a subsequent program involving juvenile delinquents (Goode 1971).

Under this program recent young college graduates were hired as police youth specialists. Their general task was to represent the department in junior high schools. Specifically, they were expected to "evaluate, examine, counsel, and care about those cases of hardcore behavioral problems, which are assigned by school guidance, visiting teachers, assistant principals and principals" (p. 92).

These police youth specialists were expected to know what help was available in the community and how one might tap such resources. The problems which they could be expected to be faced with included venereal disease, emotional stress, or even a youth from a family who needed basic information as how to go about getting food stamps.

Setting up programs for youths to learn about law enforcement work through experience and training seminars has not been confined only to police departments. Since 1969 the Putnam County sheriffs have conducted a youth (Police Cadet) program as well (Germain 1974). When one takes note of Sheriff Radnor Weizenecker's ideas about his department's approach, one can readily see a comparison between it and the police projects.

"The key principle of this program," Weizenecker points out, "is education by making them aware of the purposes of Laws and today's contemporary social problems and to channel in the proper direction the aggressiveness and anxiety of the young through youth originated activities which help serve themselves and the public welfare."

These goals, he says, are achieved by on-the-scene participation and education, by accompanying a law enforcement officer on tour, day or night, or by working along side of the desk officer who has the initial contact with the public and their problems. (Germain 1974, p. 40)

Young People Trained As Police Para-Professionals*

Miami's Threshold Program which began in 1974 offers police apprenticeships to young people from 18 to 20 years of age with the objective of recruiting them into the police force when they reach the minimum age of 21. As Public Service Aides (PSAs), these paraprofessionals perform the non-law enforcement duties which usually consume up to 75 percent of a police officer's time. With PSAs handling such duties police officers can devote more time to preventive and investigative activities.

The Threshold Program, which is funded by LEAA, is advertised in Miami through newspapers, radio, and school announcements in both English and Spanish. Program officials place special emphasis on recruiting minority group members and women as PSAs. Applicants must first pass medical, intelligence, and physical agility tests to determine their capability for police work. Those who are accepted then participate in an intensive, ten-week course at the Southeast Florida Institute of Criminal Justice where they earn nine college credits. The course of study covers such topics as basic law, patrol operations, and human relations training. Following their classroom preparation, aides participate in a seven week in-service training program at the Miami Police Department. By rotating to the various departmental units, such as homicide, robbery, and community relations, PSAs learn the basic procedures of each division. They also ride with senior police officers as observers before receiving street assignments.

As Public Service Aides, the young men and women work 30 hours

---

*From *Target*, 4(12), December 1975, pp. 1–2. Target is prepared by the International City Management Association and is described as a "Newsletter of Innovative Projects Funded by the Law Enforcement Assistance Administration."

a week at $3 an hour while pursuing an Associate Degree in Law Enforcement part-time at a local college. They are not armed and do not have arrest authority. While patroling in cars marked with special "Miami Police Public Service Aide" decals, aides communicate with their dispatcher by means of a portable radio.

Currently, there are 55 Public Service Aides. They handle approximately 200 calls a week involving such activities as directing and maintaining traffic flow at accident sites, report writing, citizen complaints, referring citizens with problems to appropriate agencies, providing aid to the sick and injured, and filing written reports on complaints called into the complaint room at headquarters.

Public Service Aides are assigned to areas which computer print-outs identify as having the highest calls for service. When they are not on call, PSAs contact businesses and residents in their assigned areas to inform them about operation identification and receive suggestions on how police services can be improved.

During the past year, PSAs have answered 80 percent of the non-enforcement type calls coming into the Miami Police Department. Of the first 40 PSAs to enter the program, seven have become police officers upon reaching their 21st birthdays.

Figure 6-2.

Even though many of the innovative youth-police projects were initiated in the late 1960s and early 1970s announcement of new ones are still being made (see Fig. 6-2). Whether continued efforts in this area will continue into the next decade remains to be seen. However, one things seems evident. The old police athletic league concept of having several officers coach the local team and play with the area youth to win them over is no longer considered to be sufficient. The time has come for more ambitious, creative youth programs. To deny this in light of what we now know and have seen in previous projects would be unfortunate, particularly now when the crime problem continues to plague society and capture many of its youth.

Figure 6-3. Public Service Aides (police paraprofessionals) completing a motor vehicle report. (Photo courtesy of Miami Police Department.)

Citizen Involvement

In the past decade a good deal of publicity has been devoted to how the lack of citizen involvement and cooperation has made the job of the police officer harder. In response to this situation, most departments have initiated police-community relations programs. In this pursuit, some have even sought to actively get citizens to experience police work itself.

One such effort at increasing the level of understanding of police work was undertaken by the City of Carpinteria, California, P.D. (Eliason 1970). In this unique "Citizen on Patrol" (C.O.P.) program, citizens over the age of thirteen years of age were permitted to ride with a regular officer during specified hours.

The citizen riders included businessmen, as well as college and high school students. They were in a position to answer radio calls and, in some cases, actually assist the officer when danger was not an issue.

In addressing his comments to fellow officers, Sergeant Kevin Eliason (1970), who participated in the C.O.P. program, said, "At first there was some apprehensiveness on the part of one or two officers to the program. They felt they would be watched and criticized and that the citizen would just be in the way. It didn't take long for these doubts to be eliminated . . . They see just what you and I have to contend with in the field. They see the emotional and human side of police work, realizing also that we are only human beings . . ." (p. 33).

In contrast to the C.O.P. program and ones like it in which volunteers are given only a one-time glimpse of police work, the New York City P.D. developed a more long term program (Oliver 1973). It involved the recruitment, training, and use of civilian women as precinct receptionists.

This program was initiated because the area police station quite often proved to be the only government agency in a locale which was in a position to provide assistance—particularly in certain inner city sections during the off hours. If the gap is going to be closed rather than widen between the police and the community in such instances, the police must be willing to help people who enter the stationhouse with non-law enforcement problems. This is where the precinct receptionist fits into the picture.

She serves to greet visitors as they enter the building. If their difficulties are of a strictly police nature, they are directed to an officer. However, if the problem is one of welfare, housing, general information, or of a specifically non-police nature, the receptionist endeavors to interview the person and attempts to handle it through taking various actions. Such actions might include recommending an agency to handle the problem, becoming personally involved in making an initial phone contact, or endeavoring to make a follow-up on the initial referral to ensure the person did receive the proper attention.

Two of the positive results of the Precinct Receptionist Program were in terms of the reactions of both the community and the uniformed police officers. Initially, some of the police seemed wary of the program. They saw it, at the very least, as an invasion of their private "fortress." Eventually though, they began to see the value of having the receptionists handle technically non-police duties in terms of a savings in their own time and a lessening of their work load.

For the community's part, the stationhouse was now being

looked upon as a place for the to come when in need of assistance. "In short," to quote Sergeant John Oliver, an assistant project director of the Precinct Receptionist Program, "the precinct was now being considered a community resource."

Indigenous Paraprofessionals in Police Work

The police paraprofessional and cadet movements received a great deal of momentum by virtue of the fact that recruitment of minority group members was a prime objective of police managers. As a matter of fact, as Gartner (1971) goes so far to note, "The term, 'paraprofessional,' in police and corrections work is, in a sense, a misnomer, for few of the professionals possess college degrees, the usual, if often irrelevant, denominator of the class. More distinguishing, especially in police work, is indigenousness . . . " (p. 85).

Probably one of the key examples of the use of indigenous personnel was following the Watts Riot in Los Angeles (L.A.P.D. 1969). In this program the L.A.P.D. started to use Community Relations Aides in their police-community relations strategy. This program was particularly bold in that the case-aide group was made up of school dropouts, a majority of whom were former convicted felons. Yet, despite these background factors, they were involved in activities such as lecturing, training, and supervision in schools, community meetings, and summer programs.

POLICE AS PARAPROFESSIONALS

Up to this point the emphasis has been on the use of civilian volunteers and salaried workers to fill positions formerly held by police officers. The other aspects of the new careers movement in law enforcement has been the training of police to perform formal /informal roles previously reserved to professionals in the mental health and legal fields.

Police as "Practical Psychologists"

Interest in the actions of police officers has traditionally been confined to their law enforcement functions. Yet, the social roles they fill on the street are also quite important.

Each day law enforcement personnel are put in contact with people under emotional stress, some of whom are so pressured that they act in a bizarre or violent manner. When situations such as this arise, the police officer needs to know how to handle them (Wicks 1974a).

If a police officer acts properly he may be able to save a suicidal individual from injuring or killing himself. Also, unless a police officer is aware of certain behavioral principles and techniques, he may be unable to prevent a crowd from developing into a mob.

Family disturbance calls are one of the leading causes of police fatalities. One study estimates that they account for 40 percent of the time lost due to disabilities resulting from injuries sustained while on duty (Bard, 1970). New special training in handling marital and family disputes applying basic psychological techniques will result in fewer injuries and more lives being saved.

Training in applied psychology, human relations, ethnic awareness, interviewing, and other socially oriented subjects is no longer a luxury for peace officers. Police and correction academies are changing their curricula and including courses in interpersonal relations and other behaviorally oriented topics. Even the traditional community relations course is now receiving more attention, and recent guidelines illustrate a desire to up-date and broaden it (see Fig. 6-4).

COMMUNITY RELATIONS IN CRIMINAL JUSTICE*
Course Guideline

Catalogue Description

Problems in citizen relations; treatment of victims, witnesses, and jurors; citizen involvement in the criminal justice process; community resources related to criminal justice programming.

Selected Reading Resources

Advisory Commission on Criminal Justice Standards and Goals. *Community Crime Prevention.* Washington, D.C.: Government Printing Office, 1973.
Berkeley, George E. *The Democratic Policeman.* Boston: Beacon Press, 1969.

Brandstatter, A. F., and Louis A. Radelet. *Police-Community Relations.* Beverly Hills, California: Glencoe Press, 1968.

Coffey, Alan, Edward Eldefonso, and Walter Hartiner. *Human Relations—Law Enforcement in a Changing Community.* Englewood Cliffs, N.J.: Prentice-Hall, Inc., 1967.

Curry, J. E., and Glen D. King. *Race Tensions and the Police.* Springfield, Ill.: C. C. Thomas, 1967.

Martin, John M. *Delinquency Today: A Guide for Community Action.* Washington, D.C.: Government Printing Office, 1968.

Neiderhoffer, Arthur, and Alexander Smith. *New Directions in Police Community Relations.* San Francisco: Rinehart Press, 1974.

Portune, Robert G. *Changing Adolescent Attitude Toward Police.* Cincinnati, Ohio: W. H. Anderson Co., 1971.

Radelet, Louis A. *The Police and the Community.* Beverly Hills: Glencoe Press, 1973.

Trojanowicz, Robert C., John M. Trojanowicz, and Forrest Moss. *Community Based Crime Prevention.* Palisades, Calif.: Goodyear Publishing, 1974.

Trojanowicz, Robert C., and Samuel Dixon. *Criminal Justice and the Community.* Englewood Cliffs, N.J.: Prentice-Hall, 1974.

Course Outline

   I. Democratic justice systems
      A. The concept of community service
      B. Necessity of maintaining positive community relations
         1. Relation to crime resolution
         2. Relation to civil disobedience
      C. Implications of professionalism

  II. Citizen treatment
      A. Improving the treatment of victims and witnesses
      B. Jury selection and management
      C. Handling citizen complaints
      D. Equal treatment issues
         1. Delay in trial
         2. Plea bargaining
         3. Adequate counsel
         4. Enforcement bias

 III. Impact of social problems
      A. Urbanization and depersonalization

    B. Minority group relations
       1. The civil rights movement
       2. Barriers to effective communication
    C. Relations with the "youth community"
       1. The problem of drugs
       2. Police and juvenile court involvement in the schools
       3. Campus unrest
    D. Militant and dissident organizations
    E. Political and racial disturbances
       1. Measured reaction
       2. Role of the courts

IV. Formal community relations programming
    A. Media relations
    B. Community relations institutes
    C. Crime prevention programming
       1. Neighborhood organizations
       2. Target hardening
          a. Property identification
          b. Premise surveys
          c. Information programs
       3. Volunteers in corrections programming

V. Relations with auxiliary services
    A. Social service bureaus
    B. Educational institutions
    C. Community improvement programs
    D. Drug abuse and alcohol centers

Figure 6-4.

Colleges and community colleges are responding as well. They are changing criminal justice programs to include more social science courses. Many colleges, including Northern Virginia Community College and St. John's University of New York, have developed specific applied psychology courses for police officers (Wicks 1974c).

The movement to educate criminal justice line officers in the

*Source: Hoover, Larry T.:   *Police Educational Characteristics and Curricula.* U.S. Department of Justice, U.S. Government Printing Office, Washington, D.C., 1975.

behavioral sciences can have a significant positive impact. This is reflected in the continued use of police units assigned to such delicate interpersonal activities as intervening in marital disputes and interviewing rape victims.

However, if such progress is to continue, training efforts must be updated in psychology so the information given is less general and more relevant. In the past, some officers have looked upon human relations training as unreal and unimportant to the officer in the street. In certain cases such negative reactions have been deserved; the psychology course given to officers has often centered on theories too distant and difficult to apply.

> This situation should be rectified; the officer who is called upon to serve as a "practical psychologist" in the street and on the prison tier should be able to gain a good deal from the behavioral sciences. Accordingly, along with attempting to determine those areas of importance to criminal justice officers, the psychology instructor teaching officers should take a number of minimal steps to improve his course, such as:
> - Discarding the general psychology model and replacing it with an applied version.
> - Integrating (whenever possible) experienced police/correctional trainers into the training modality.
> - Using a group-process method to supplement the didactic approach traditionally used. (Wicks, 1974c, p. 65)

Police Legal Paraprofessional

Just as it is important to get useful psychological information into the life line of the police precinct, it is also essential to have legal assistance available to officers at the local level. Especially today when rights, laws, and legal issues affect many of the actions that police take or fail to perform, legal advice is essential to the line officer.

Though many police departments have attorneys who are in their employ, such legal support is not sufficient. Legal advice is often needed quickly and locally. A central office of legal affairs is frequently unable to be responsive enough.

In recognition of this situation, the Capital University Law School has assisted the Columbus Ohio Police Department in turning officers into new sources of legal manpower. Through an intensive summer course and subsequent academic work during the normal college year, officers were trained to understand basic legal issues and processes. In this way they would be in a special position, as persons already familiar with police work and department procedures, to be of assistance to the department (Palmer 1973).

Final Comments

To typecast the police paraprofessional merely as an extender of the officer's role is not sufficient. New careerists are in a position to transform the stationhouse into a real community resource. Particularly in the case of the indigenous paraprofessional, there is a good chance that with this person one can bring the community back into the stationhouse and re-establish the local law enforcement agency as a part of the community.

As well as offering human services assistance, police paraprofessionals can also aid in the law enforcement function of the police. Indirectly, they accomplish this by aiding in the improvement of police-community relations, and by freeing more time for the officer by relieving him from becoming involved in many routine chores.

Relations with the community have been strained, especially in the past several decades. By putting a member of the community in the stationhouse, two factors can result: (1) the people will feel less threatened about going to the stationhouse for help and even may begin to identify it as a resource, and (2) if the stationhouse's image can be changed from negative (it's a place where you get booked, fingerprinted, and jailed) to positive, the community may be more willing to cooperate and support the police in their daily functions.

Also, if police can be relieved of some of the daily clerical and administrative chores, more time will be loosened up for more appropriate work. The fear that *all* police work had to be done by uniformed personnel is a myth that the new careers movement has attacked. Civilians can be involved in basic tasks, technical roles, such as crime scene photography, or social service roles.

One danger inherent in the paraprofessional movement in this setting is that the police will seek to give up and delegate all social service-type activities. It is a good idea to participate in a joint effort with civilians to create a broader, more efficient police department. However, if hiring civilians means shirking all duties except strictly law enforcement ones, the police will end up with nothing but a limited, militaristic role which will be alien to the very people being protected.

While such a role may be appropriate for an officer involved in a special security mission, it is not the role for the street officer or even the investigator, who needs to ineract with people and gain their confidence as a public servant. The line officers need to know and appreciate the service functions they must perform, as the service functions and the enforcement functions go hand in hand.

Officers are often put into positions where they must be able to recognize and diffuse potentially volatile situations. To accomplish this effectively they must begin to see themselves as crisis interveners as well as law enforcement specialists. Police often serve in many instances as "practical psychologists"; therefore, the effects to improve their expertise in the area of human behavior through specialized psychology training is a worthwhile idea.

REFERENCES

Bard, Morton: *Training Police as Specialists in Family Crisis Intervention.* U.S. Department of Justice, U.S. Government Printing Office, Washington, D.C., 1970.

Caplan, Gerald: Foreword. In *Employing Civilians for Police Work.* U.S. Department of Justice, U.S. Government Printing Officer, Washington, D.C., 1975, p. vi.

Eliason, Keven D.: Citizens on patrol. *Law and Order, 18(11),* 32-33, 1970.

Gartner, Alan: *Paraprofessionals and Their Performance.* Praeger, New York, 1971.

Germain, Fred: Teen police learn and lend a hand. *Law and Order, 22(5),* 40-42, 1974.

Goode, John E.: A juvenile delinquency demonstration project. *Law and Order, 19(5),* 92-93, 1971.

Goode, John E.: Police youth patrol pilot. *Law and Order, 18(3),* 34-41, 1970.

Los Angeles Police Department: *An Interim Evaluation of the Community Relations Aides' Performance in the Community Relations Program.*

LAPD, Los Angeles, 1969.

Nemetz, W. C.: How trained assistants increase effective police power. *Police Chief, 40*(1), 20, 64, 1973.

Oliver, John P.: Paraprofessionals: the precinct receptionist program. *Police Chief, 40*(1), 40-41, 1973.

Schwartz, Alfred I., Vaughn, Alease M., Waller, John D., and Wholey, Joseph S.: *Employing Civilians for Police Work.* U.S. Department of Justice, U.S. Government Printing Office, Washington, D.C., 1975.

Social Development Corporation: *Use of Manpower in a City Police Force: A Model Based on a Study of the Fremont, California, Police Department.* Bethesda, Maryland, 1973.

Treback, Arnold and Idelson, Evelyn: *New Careers in Justice: A Status Report.* National Institute of New Careers, Washington, D.C., 1970.

Wicks, Robert J.: *Applied Psychology for Law Enforcement and Correction Officers.* McGraw-Hill, New York, 1974a.

———: Presenting psychological concepts to police and correction officers. *Police Chief, 41*(11), 65, 1974b.

———: Professionalization of the criminal justice line officer: implications for curriculum design. *Technical Education News, 35*(1), 12-13, 1974c.

Chapter 7

COURTS*

A GOOD DEAL OF POWER resides in the courts. This is an obvious reality. A judge can induce change where none was thought possible. (This became especially evident in the case of desegregation.)

Yet, while judges have been able to order institutions, offenders, and issues to be corrected, until recently they have seemed powerless to produce major changes in their own system. Backlogged court calendars, delays of probation reports, and the presence of an overwhelming amount of work for judges have long plagued the court system. While this situation is largely unchanged today, efforts are at least now being made to achieve some positive alteration of the situation.

Volunteers and nonprofessionals are being sought—as they once were in the past—to fill roles as court workers and assistant probation/community officers. Essentially, these efforts are being made in order to—

1. Relieve the present justices of their heavy workloads through the use of parajudges.

2. Divert juveniles from the criminal justice system before they get enmeshed in it and begin a vicious cycle of crime.

3. Provide enough citizen probation personnel so that alternatives to incarceration are more feasible.

VOLUNTEERS IN THE COURTS

In general, the movement toward utilization of volunteers in the courts has to be viewed positively for the great potential good such a step offers. However, as Ivan Scheier (1970), Director of The National Information Center on Volunteers in Courts, recognizes, a court volunteer program can fail despite the enthusiasm

---

*See also Appendix 7.

103

of the workers and the fact that other agencies have successfully employed nonsalaried personnel.

> The surging growth of the modern court volunteer movement pre-disposes fixation on quantity. Thus, at least a thousand courts use volunteers, at this writing, 50-75 new ones each month, 40-50 thousand court volunteers at work today, etc. Yet in the end, quality matters more; it is rare enough today. Possibly one in twenty court volunteer programs have reached anywhere near their full human potential. After the first rush of enthusiasm, the others struggle along at quarter-power, glossing over their difficulties, perhaps, but not knowing what to do about them.
>
> The unfulfilled court volunteer program can fail for the following reasons: (1) poor quality volunteers; (2) poor quality leadership; and (3) both of these. (Scheier 1970, P. 1)

There are many reasons for failure in setting up and administering a court volunteer program. Many of them are applicable to the development of a volunteer organization under any circumstances, rather than being just germane to the court setting. Nevertheless, the key reasons for the failure of a court volunteer program include the following:

1. Discontinuous recruitment process.
2. Inadequate screening procedures for potential volunteers.
3. Inappropriate management.
4. Insufficient training.
5. Lack of supervision.
6. Poor leadership in the volunteer ranks.
7. Absence of—or the presence of a less than adequate number of—full-time, paid directors and program coordinators.
8. Acceptance of a vaguely conceived notion of how to employ volunteers.
9. Failure to develop a job ladder which allows for experienced volunteers, as well as new ones possessing professional talents, to fill responsible positions commensurate with their skills and experience.

One of the major problems cited by Scheier in his analysis of the process of incorporating volunteers in the courts, centers on the organizational difficulties within the existing court staff itself.

Without an effective organization designed to deal with volunteers, the program can often turn out to be a failure from the start or end up being an example of inadequate tokenism.

Scheier sees the failure of the courts to delegate leadership functions to volunteers when the situation warrants it as a primary block to effective volunteer utilization. He describes a number of possibilities in which leadership delegation can be set up as a model in the court system (see Fig. 7-1).

Some models permit no delegation of program management, i.e. one-track model (see "D" in Fig. 7-1), while other court management styles encourage almost total self-direction ("A" in Fig. 7-1). Scheier suggests that while the style employed depends on the court's individual situation, it is important for the court to be consciously aware of the available forms of management and the illustrations and precedents for each of them. In this way one can be chosen which is most appropriate, so that tokenism (in which only a few volunteers are used) or haphazardous application of nonsalaried workers does not turn out to be the unfortunate, logical result of a volunteer program in the courts.

Lay Magistrates in England

One of the ways in which volunteers and paraprofessionals are being actively employed in the court system is as parajudges. "Parajudge" is a term which will be used interchangeably here with "magistrate" and "justice of the peace" (JP). The use of non-lawyer judges is again becoming popular in the United States. However, across the Atlantic in England more than 98 percent of all criminal cases are tried before lay judges in magistrate courts.

> Except for approximately 50 full time professional stipendiaries (most of whom sit in London) who are former solicitors or barristers, all of the 20,600 magistrates who sit in England and Wales are unpaid lay persons who donate their time. They sit in benches of three for 26 days each year in more than 900 courts, and they are the backbone of the criminal justice system. Even the most serious crimes pass through these courts, for it is here, since the abolition of the Grand Jury in 1933, that committal proceedings are held to make certain that there is sufficient evidence to warrant sending a case to Crown Court . . . In addition to criminal cases, magistrates also hear juvenile and family cases. (Reichert 1973, P. 138)

THE ONE-TRACK (UNDELEGATED) VS. THE TWO-TRACK (DELEGATED) MODEL OF COURT VOLUNTEER PROGRAM MANAGEMENT

In the accompanying diagram the function is considered *integrated* where the circle is within the square, thus ☐0. It is considered to be performed by a group which is *separate* (an auxilliary) from the court when the two figures are separate, thus ☐0.

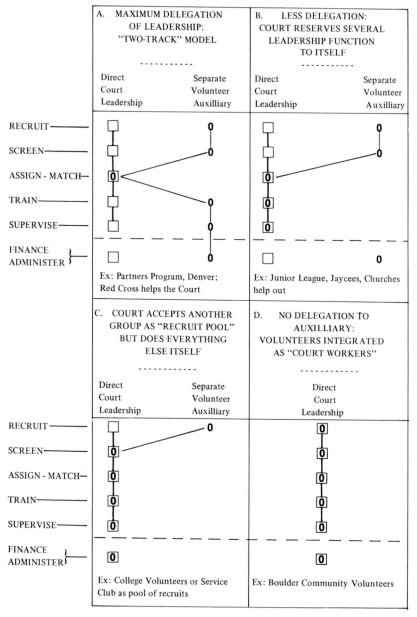

Figure 7-1. The one-track (undelegated) vs. the two-track (delegated) model of court volunteer program management.

In theory, anyone can become a magistrate in England. People are actually chosen for the post when the Lord Chancellor selects their names from a list presented by a local advisory committee. This committee makes a special effort to develop a list which represents a cross section of the community.

The use of magistrates is not without its critics. The primary objection to the use of non-lawyers is that the use of only professionals avoids the inconsistencies in sentencing that they believe arise when "unqualified" magistrates sit on the bench. However, Irving F. Reichert, who was in England under a Ford Foundation grant for the expressed purpose of exploring aspects of the criminal justice system in that country, argues with these critics.

Reichert indicates that even a brief examination of the sentencing of the professional judiciary will demonstrate that inconsistencies are just as evident when the judge is a lawyer. Also, Reichert notes that lay magistrates may possess a broader base of knowledge than their professional counterparts. As a matter of fact, in England, lay justices must visit the penal institution to which they send a convicted offender—something that, unfortunately, judges in England and the United States, who are deemed professionals, are not usually required to do.

To further counter criticism of the parajudges, there has been a compulsory training program for them since 1966. Such a step should provide a model for the United States to examine as a part of their overall effort to increase the use of non-legally trained laymen to handle judicial matters.

Parajudges in the United States

The Federal Magistrate's Act of 1968 authorized U.S. district judges to employ lay magistrates to conduct some pre-trial hearings, try minor offenses, and to act as special masters. Since this ruling many states and municipalities have begun to turn to an expanded use of paraprofessionals.

This move toward employment of parajudges is supported by members of the judiciary as well as citizen groups. This is illustrated in the following comments by Irving R. Kaufman, a judge of the United States Court of Appeals:

I see two basic benefits from greater use of paraprofessionals in our courts. First, we could at last make a dent in court congestion and delays. Second, we could do it relatively inexpensively. Simply creating more judgeships to cope with increased court business is a long, expensive, frustrating, and often inefficient procedure for reducing court congestion. It has been estimated that it costs about $25,000 to make a single federal judge operational, and continuing yearly expenses for salary, staff, and supporting services run to about $200,000 a year. While it may be somewhat fairer to relate increased judgeships to increased trial days, nonetheless, in 1961 when judicial manpower was increased 26% in the federal district courts, civil dispositions showed only a disappointing 13% rise, while criminal dispositions rose but 5%. (Kaufman 1970, pp. 147-48)

Justice Kaufman believes paraprofessionals can aid the courts in two primary ways. It can relieve the judges of many routine tasks so that they can be more free to write opinions and conduct trials. He also sees the use of parajudges in pre-trial hearings and motions as extremely valuable since these processes take up such a major portion of a judge's time today.

Handling traffic offenses is one particular type of work a parajudge can easily handle. In 1970, New York City transferred most of the processing of traffic and parking offenses from the jurisdiction of the judge to the trial examiners. These examiners are not paraprofessionals in the true sense of the word as they are drawn from the local bar association. However, they do show the direction in which the court system is moving—namely, away from a strict use of only trained professional justices at every stage of a court proceeding with every type of offense.

Another step in the move away from law degreed justices is the increasing and further systematizing of the justice-of-the-peace program. In Montana this process has been supported by state legislation. It also involves the initiation of a training course for justices of the peace at the University of Montana and receipt by justices of the peace of more assistance from the state in the establishment of regular salaries (Brownlee 1975). These steps are not unusual, considering that speedy justice would be impossible in a rural state like Montana where some counties boast of having only one lawyer in residence.

Iowa has taken a different approach to the problem of a shortage of decision makers in the judiciary. In the state's Unified Trial Court Act of 1972 they sought to strengthen administrative coordination and supervision of the lower courts, while improving efficiency.

Iowa did this by having special county judicial magistrate commissions appoint new judicial magistrates who would have responsibilities and powers similar to the old justices of the peace. The reported results of the act were (Green, Ross and Schmidhausen 1975) as follows:

1. Replacement of
   (a) 515 justice of the peace courts
   (b) 899 mayor's courts
   (c) 34 police courts
   (d) 14 municipal courts
2. Employment of higher trained personnel (47.2% lawyers) comprised of
   (a) 196 part-time judicial magistrates
   (b) 5 full-time magistrates
   (c) 24 associate district court judges
3. An average increase in the processing of cases (over the formerly loosely supervised justices of the peace) of 55 percent.

No studies have yet shown how effective the non-lawyers in this group of Iowan magistrates have proved to be in comparison with the lawyers. However, one point that can be taken from this realignment of services and the elimination of the justices of the peace is that even the useful JP positions become wasteful if supervision is lacking.

In the future use of parajudges—particularly non-lawyers—optimism must be 'tempered by careful planning and a full attention given to establishing guidelines regarding the limits beyond which their use would be inappropriate. As Jeffrey Parness, a research assistant from the American Judicature Society, notes,

> It is apparent that without proper court supervision, the burden on litigants with respect to their constitutional rights to a jury trial may become too onerous. Parajudicial personnel can only avoid conflict with federal and state constitutional rights to a jury trial if their

powers are appropriately defined and limited by the courts which employ them. (Parness 1974, P. 55)

Court Workers

As well as parajudges, there are court programs which employ volunteers and new careerists in other roles. One of these roles is as a Juvenile Court Service Officer.

In New York City a program designed to employ such workers was initiated in 1967 (Dohen 1971). It was established by a private city-wide poverty agency, the Puerto Rican Community Development Project.

The primary goal of this program was to employ nonprofessional Puerto Rican court workers to help youths of the same ethnic background who were brought into the juvenile section of the New York City Family Court. The nine females and three male workers between the ages of twenty and sixty who were employed did not possess a college degree. In the eighteen months they operated in the program, they handled approximately 1300 cases.

Regarding their roles, Dohen (1971) notes that the "court workers developed their multifaceted role in what seemed to be a typically Puerto Rican way. They shunned advocacy, which would have involved confrontation with court representatives, and instead inserted themselves into the court. However, they were not assimilationists. They kept their Puerto Rican identity . . . " (p. 26).

The key functions these court workers performed were as case finders, cross-cultural interpreters representers of the Puerto Rican social environment, and as intermediaries between their community and New York City agencies. As case finders they received referrals in a field office from schools, police, and other community representatives, as well as through making contacts with youths during the intake after a youth's entry into the juvenile term of the Family Court. As an interpreter and representative of the Puerto Rican social environment, the worker was not just serving to bridge the language barrier between the youth, his family, and the court, the worker was also seeking to help everyone involved to understand each other better.

The program gave the workers a chance to help the court personnel understand such elements as Puerto Rican cultural patterns and social mores. To the juvenile's family, this program functioned, in part, as a guide to the purpose and operation of the court so misunderstandings or alienation and fear in dealing with the judicial staff or the court's procedures could be avoided.

In some cases, as in the following one, intervention on the part of the worker seemed to help the parents realize what the court could and could not do here in the United States.

> One parent, following a custom developed, in small-town Puerto Rico, wanted to bring his child to court for minor infractions of parental rules. In Puerto Rico, the judge would have given the misbehaving child a tongue-lashing and sent him home. The court worker told the parent about the situation in New Your City courts, explained what would be the effects of a formal complaint against the child in a Person in Need of Supervision (PINS) petition, and convinced him that the child's misbehavior needed no such drastic measures. (Dohen 1971, P. 26)

Another New York program which sought to utilize nonprofessionals who spoke "the language of the street and community" was the Manhattan Court Employment Project. In this instance the workers or "reps," as they were called, consisted of a group of ex-offenders who were employed "to intervene in the usual court process just after a defendant's arrest, to offer him counseling and job opportunities, and if he cooperated and appeared to show promise of permanent change, to recommend that the prosecutor and the judge dismiss the charge against him without ever deciding whether he is guilty" (Vera Institute of Justice 1970, p. 7).

Training Court Volunteers

One of the key elements of the Manhattan Court Employment Project as well as of a similar Washington, D.C., program (Project Crossroads) is the training of nonprofessional personnel involved in the operation. As the report from the latter program recognized the effectiveness of the paraprofessional worker, they also note further that "it is a fallacy to assume that *any* indigenous, noncredentialed worker can perform at a high level of proficiency without training or supervision" (Lieberg 1971, p. 8).

This point has already been discussed in the chapter on training of new careerists and volunteers. There seems to be no question that indigenousness of itself is not a factor which eliminates the need for additional training and guarantees success with the target population of the program.

The need for training of volunteers who are not indigenous is possibly more obvious. Considering this need, a number of workers have suggested formats for their training. James Jorgensen (1969), for example, provided one model for training volunteers who wished to work in the juvenile institutional program, which he feels can also be modified for use in training adult court workers.

His course was based on several assumptions:

1. Volunteers are unfamiliar with the life styles of delinquents or the systemic factors which give rise to delinquency.

2. Those who offer their services do not appreciate the actual ways in which society deals with delinquency today.

3. Volunteers need to become familiar with the issues involved in the psychology of delinquency and how deviant, maladaptive youth behavior is *learned*.

4. Volunteers do not fully appreciate the positive impact they can make.

With these propositions as a backdrop, Jorgensen's model was designed to eliminate myths and simplistic attitudes held by prospective, nonindigenous volunteers. He recommended such actions as on-site visits by the trainees to high delinquency neighborhoods and juvenile institutions, as well as observing juvenile officers at work.

Other elements in the course were group discussions and lectures on juvenile typology, differential treatment (matching treatment to the individual delinquent), and counseling. This training program, as in others directed at preparing volunteers for therapeutic intervention work, was designed then to (1) destroy misconceptions, (2) increase sensitivity to the real problems and causal factors of the target population, and (3) provide a basic understanding of how one can function as an agent of change.

VOLUNTEERS AND NONPROFESSIONALS
IN PROBATION AND PAROLE

In the past ten years, studies have shown that even the most advanced juvenile correction program rarely prove to be the most advantageous means to treating delinquents. Consequently, many reformers have decided that less action and interference on the part of the criminal justice system to deal with juveniles would be to everyone's best interest.

In other words, many professionals seemed to have the feeling that corrective efforts were proving to have little or no positive results, and that it was time for the system to use every diversion technique at its disposal. In essence, the rule of thumb today seems to be "judicious nonintervention" or "leave the kids alone whenever possible" (Schur 1973, pp. 154-55).

Accordingly, there has been a general move toward keeping juveniles out of institutions. This can be accomplished through the use of diversionary techniques prior to processing by the courts. Also, it can be achieved through an increase in the utilization of probation and parole.

The only problem with such a move, though, has been the extremely understaffed program conducted by the probation and parole departments. (Often probation and parole operations are run by the same department—sometimes in close conjunction with the court.) So, it is no wonder that the use of nonprofessionals (including exoffenders) and volunteers is a most logical alternative to personnel shortage in these agencies.

> Probation must get out of the country doctor era and into the age of the clinic. We can no longer waste the training of probation officers on inappropriate tasks. We are less in need of extra probation officers than we are in need of a corps of auxiliary workers to spread the effect of the officers we already have. (Loughery 1969, P. 247)

The use of nonprofessionals is not a new or exclusively United States experiment. In 1841, John Augustus, a Boston cobbler, began using volunteers as probation personnel. Today, part-time and full-time nonprofessionals and volunteers are in evidence in hundreds of U.S. courts. Additionally, other nations are also experimenting with employment of these types of workers.

In Kyoto prefecture in Japan, for example, there are at least one thousand volunteer probation officers. They are not only involved in routine tasks, but are also actually responsible for most supervision of probationers (Hogan 1971).

Students have also been involved successfully in a number of probation projects. Anderson College students in one Indiana program, for example, were recruited to work with probationers. These summer internships were set up to see if probationers would relate better to younger workers and also to expose these college volunteers to work in the criminal justice field (Clear 1971).

A similar program was set up by the U.S. Probation and Parole Office in Chicago. However, the paraprofessionals used in this case were not college students, but indigenous nonprofessionals (some of whom were exoffenders), lacking any large measure of advanced training.

As the Anderson College program was designed as a method of eliciting interest on the part of college students, the Chicago experiment was set up partially with the belief that "the paraprofessional position in corrections could serve as an entry point to a career line for blacks and members of other minority groups with potential advancement to professional status contingent upon good performance, additional training, and achievement of an academic degree" (University of Chicago 1970, p. 15).

Two approaches which have been cited as "exemplary projects" by the Law Enforcement Assistance Administration in the area of probation and parole are *The Lincoln, Nebraska, Volunteer Probation Counselor Program* and *The Ohio Parole Officer Aide Program.*

Volunteer Probation Counselor Program

In Lincoln, Nebraska, an example of community involvement in the probation setting is a program where lay volunteers are being assigned to counsel high-risk probationers, i.e. ones who are misdemeanants of ages sixteen to twenty-five with an average of 7.3 previous arrests and convictions.

This program has a number of features which, it is believed, have aided in making it workable. These key aspects center around the careful attention given to volunteer screening, training, and matching.

Unlike some loosely organized court volunteer programs, the one in Lincoln, Nebraska, is set up so that those persons with undesirable/unrealistic motivations and few personal resources are not accepted. For instance, applicants who are burdened with their own emotional problems cannot spend enough time with the probationers, or are considered gullible, faddish, domineering, or vengeful are not considered appropriate.

Information about the volunteer candidate is obtained via a formal application (see Appendix 7). The thorough screening of the candidate also picks up further material during the interviews with the volunteer coordinator and from the psychological testing.

The training is devoted primarily to enhancing the volunteer's counseling and crisis intervention skills. Though the initial educational program consists of eight hours of instruction during three evening sessions, his training informally continues via supervision received while on the job. Observation during training and while working as a volunteer serves to provide the program coordinator with further information on the person's continued ability to be an effective helping agent.

The matching process is concerned with determining what type of relationship the probationer needs and then assigning him to the volunteer with the personal skills and background most suitable to provide what is needed in the particular case in question. Within the Lincoln program four general types of relationships are defined: role model, friend/companion, supervisor/custodian, and primary counselor.

Though these model relationships have been arbitrarily named, they demonstrate a recognition that juveniles often require different treatment in response to their individual needs. For example, in the "friend/companion" relationship, it has been determined that the probationer is a bit of a rebel and has a hard time relating to peers and authority figures. In this case, the volunteer chosen is someone who is slightly older but who is compatible with the probationer in terms of interests and types of activities usually performed.

The directors may also feel that some probationers have few resources and need an older, more mature person to supervise them and guide them in their day to day living (job seeking, finances). In this situation, a different type of volunteer would be chosen and matched to the client. In other words, the treatment in the program is differential; the mode and agent of support is matched to the probationer according to his needs. As one might note, in order to accomplish this, the program needs to have a group of volunteers with varied skills and backgrounds.

During their interactions with the youths, the volunteer counselors are expected to keep progress sheets (see Fig. 7-2). These reports help the directors as counselors themselves to monitor the probationer's progress. They aid as well in helping the volunteer and his supervisor to determine if the matching process has been successful or needs some modification.

In respect to progress of the program in general, a one-year comparative analysis of recidivism (the tendency to relapse into criminal behavior) in the Lincoln program and a control regular probation program showed these results:

	Percent of Recidivism	
	Volunteer	*Control*
New nontraffic offenses	15	63.7
Multiple new offenses	10	52.2

A further analysis of the criminal offenses committed during the period one year prior to probation and during the probationary year also shows positive results for the program (see Table 7-I). Accordingly, the program at the very least further emphasizes the need to continue experimenting with different, more creative—yet organized—methods of utilizing volunteers in working with (even difficult) probationers.

The Ohio Parole Officer Aide Program

In 1976, The Parole Officer Aide Program of Ohio was one of seventeen programs which earned the National Institute of Law Enforcement and Criminal Justice's "Exemplary" label. Just as

TABLE 7-I

CRIMINAL OFFENSES COMMITTED DURING THE PERIOD ONE YEAR PRIOR TO PROBATION AND DURING THE PROBATIONARY YEAR*

	High Risk						Low Risk		
	Volunteer Program (n=40)			Regular Probation (n=44)			(n=20)		
Offenses	Year Before	During	Percent Reduction	Year Before	During	Percent Reduction	Year Before	During	Percent Reduction
Theft-related	14	1	93%	11	21	(91%)†	0	1	(—)
Anti-social	29	7	76%	16	25	(56%)	4	0	100%
Alcohol-Drug	31	9	71%	31	13	58%	6	1	83%
Major traffic	51	16	68%	48	30	38%	30	3	90%
Minor traffic	25	24	4%	23	26	(13%)	8	0	100%
Totals	150	57	62.0%	129	115	10.9%	48	5	89.8%

Based on these results, the program is extremely cost-effective. The volunteers are obtained at no expense beyond the time required to recruit, train, and supervise them. In Lincoln, this amounts to approximately 350 hours per year for 77 volunteers, or about 12 percent of total probation staff time. From all indications, this small investment has yielded substantial dividends for the probationer, the criminal justice system, and the community.

*Ku, Richard: *The Volunteer Probation Counselor Program.* U.S. Government Printing Office, Washington, D.C., 1975.
†( ) indicates an *increase*.

VOLUNTEER PROBATION COUNSELOR'S
MONTHLY PROGRESS REPORT

(Due on or before 5th of month)

Volunteer_____ Probationer_____ Month_____

MEETINGS:

Total number of meetings scheduled and kept:_____

Were any meetings missed?_____If so, why and how did you handle it?_____

Use of Meetings

(1) Discussion: (Please check)
    (a) _____ Get acquainted   (c) _____ Problem oriented
    (b) _____ General discussion   (d) _____ Personal material
    (e) Other_____

(2) Special Activities (Please explain)
    (a) Recreational_____
    (b) Home Visit_____
    (c) Other_____

(3) Emergencies: (Please explain)
    (a) _____ Probationer in jail_____
    (b) _____ Reports violation of probation_____
    (c) _____ Involved in law breaking _____
    (d) _____ Family problems_____
    (e) _____ Personal problems_____

How was the emergency handled?_____

If Probation Department was consulted, were you satisfied with their handling of the problem?

AGENCY CONTACTS

What community agencies, if any, did you contact for assistance?_____

Was satisfactory service obtained?_____

THE RELATIONSHIP

Cooperative	:	:	:	:	:	:	Uncooperative
Sincere	:	:	:	:	:	:	Manipulative
Hostile	:	:	:	:	:	:	Friendly
Honest	:	:	:	:	:	:	Dishonest
Unresponsive	:	:	:	:	:	:	Responsive
Trusts me	:	:	:	:	:	:	Does not trust me

Figure 7-2a.

PROBLEMS IN THE RELATIONSHIP

(1) a. ____ No problems

b. ____ A few minor problems

c. ____ Major problems:

1. ____ Did not keep appointments

2. ____ Attendance is irregular

3. ____ Seems very aloof and distant

4. ____ Poor attitude toward society

5. ____ Does not accept advice

6. ____ Does not follow through on things we talk about and plan

7. ____ Does not seem to be forming a satisfactory relationship

(2) Are his future plans realistic?_____

(3) Future directions in the relationship:

(a) The primary problem we must work on:_____

(b) Progress to date has been:

____ Minimal ____ Slight ____ About as expected ____ Good ____ Excellent

(c) Progress since last monthly report:

____ Minimal ____ Slight ____ About as expected ____ Good ____ Excellent

Check here if you would like the probation staff to contact you regarding your probationer.

ADDITIONAL COMMENTS:_____

Figure 7-2a—7-2b. Sample form to be filled out monthly by a volunteer probation counselor showing the progress of a probationer. Source: Ku, Richard: *The Volunteer Probation Counselor Program.* U.S. Government Printing Office, Washington, D.C., 1975, pp. 113–14.

the previously discussed program in Lincoln, Nebraska, this program was evaluated and determined to be effective in reducing crime/improving criminal justice, being adaptable to other jurisdictions, producing achievement of desirable goals, and demonstrating significant cost effectiveness.

Unlike the Lincoln program, this program deals with parolees instead of probationers, and in lieu of volunteers taken from a cross section of the community, the workers in the Ohio project are salaried ex-offenders. Yet, the two programs are alike in that they both demonstrate an organized attempt to utilize nonprofessionals in correctional work with people not being institutionalized.

The Parole Officer Aide (POA) is selected and trained on the job for about six months to reach a level of expertise where he can help the parole department in many capacities. Some of his duties are to supervise parolees, speak at schools and in prisons, and aid in the development of job resources.

Considering the POA's background, he is in a position to empathize with the client and bring back unique insights to the officers he works with in the department. This advantage of using ex-offenders is not just something accepted by Ohio. As of 1974, sixteen states used ex-offenders in their parole systems. Probably the notable point about Ohio is that they are demonstrating a special desire to scrutinize their program, are offering it as a model for other states to adopt (see Fig. 7-3), and are even building in a career ladder so ex-offenders can work themselves into the role of parole officer from their point of departure as POA's. Such commitment to openness and willingness to be examined are especially helpful if we are to determine more accurately how effective various human services approaches are in the court setting, which directly includes the areas of probation and parole.

THE CHALLENGE:
Will it Work for You?*

Using the Ohio experience as a model, can other states develop POA programs in which ex-offenders are assigned major parole responsibilities?

There are strong indications the program will indeed work elsewhere. Let's look at some specific questions you may be asking.

Q. How would the program affect my normal process of selecting parole officers?

A. Like Ohio, most states would be able to establish a separate career ladder for the POA without upsetting the established PO selection system. The POA should have a career ladder which feeds into the normal parole officer selection process.

Q. How am I certain to select the best (low-risk) POAs?

A. Ohio shies away from persons younger than 22; insists that applicants successfully complete parole and be employed for six months after the completion date. Applicants can't have assaultive crime records and must be free of psycho-pathological tendencies. And they must pass a credit check.

Q. Suppose my POs are unionized?

A. Initially, the union could be a barrier. But the existence of a union means the program could be bargained for. Once the bargain is struck, the union system will formalize the program more quickly.

Q. How much does the project cost?

A. In Fiscal 1974, the Ohio POA program was supported by an LEAA grant of $329,913. The budget provided for 24 POAs (salary and benefits), consultant services, travel and supplies.

Q. How does the POA program affect case assignment?

A. Cases can be assigned in the normal manner to POs and POAs alike. Naturally, unrealistically difficult cases shouldn't go to a POA until he's had solid case experience.

Q. What about affirmative action statutory or executive mandates?

A. They make it easier to hire and promote minority and female POA candidates.

Q. How accessible is information on the Ohio program?

A. The procedures are well documented, and the Ohio Adult Parole Authority welcomes inquiries.

*Source: *Only Ex-Offenders Need Apply, The Ohio Parole Officer Aide Program.* U.S. Department of Justice, U.S. Government Printing Office, 1975.

Figure 7-3.

Final Comments

An obvious area for the paraprofessional movement is the court setting. Yet, implementation of innovative judicial and probation volunteer and paraprofessional programs is not easy. Court work is sensitive; the population of offenders, as well as the community to which they are to be returned, are sensitive to efforts which are aimed at meting out justice to the convicted.

Training programs and the willingness to accept the value of citizens guiding fellow (imprisoned) citizens need to be advanced to the point where there is a greater recognition of the new careerist's value. Just throwing volunteers into the role of probation officer would be a disservice to both the client and the community.

Similarly, resisting experimentation with nonprofessionals in the judicial system is both foolish and reactionary. If anything, this haloed part of our criminal justice system needs a breath of fresh air in the form of more public involvement. To turn our back on those in other professions who can help by giving of their time and common sense and to shirk off the potential value of adding ex-offenders, volunteers, and indigenous paraprofessionals to our aftercare force would be to accept entrenchment in lieu of potential progress in the judicial system.

REFERENCES

Beless, Donald W. and Pilcher, William S.: *Second Progress Report (July 1, 1969-June 1, 1970) of the Probation Officer-Case Aide Project.* University of Chicago, Center for the Study of Criminal Justice, Chicago, 1970.

Brownless, E. Gardner: The revival of the justice of the peace in Montana. *Judicature, 58*(8), 372-79, 1975.

Clear, Val: *Summer Profeation Internship Program 1971 (Final Report).* Anderson College, Anderson, Indiana, 1971.

Dohen, Dorothy: A new juvenile court role in an ethnically controlled community agency. *Social Work, 16*(2), 25-29, 1971.

Green, Justin, Ross, Russel M., and Schmidhauser: Iowa's magistrate system: the aftermath of reform. *Judicature, 58*(8), 380-89, 1975.

Hogan, M. H.: Probation in Japan. *Probation, 17*(1), 8-11, 1971.

Lieberg, Leon G.: *Project Crossroads: A Final Report to the Manpower Administration.* U.S. Department of Labor, U.S. Government Printing Office, Washington, D.C., 1971.

Loughery, D. L. Jr.: Innovations in probation management. *Crime and Delinquency, 15*(2), 247-58, 1969.

Parness, Jeffrey A.: The parajudge—oiling the wheels of justice. *Trial, 10*(2), 54-56, 1974.

Scheier, Ivan H.: *Incorporating Volunteers in the Courts.* National Information Center on Volunteers in the Courts, 1970.

Schur, E.: *Radical Non-Intervention: Rethinking the Delinquency Problem.* Prentice-Hall, Englewood Cliffs, New Jersey, 1973.

Vera Institute of Justice: *The Manhattan Court Employment Project of the Vera Institute of Justice, Summary Report on Phase One: Nov. 1, 1967-Oct. 31, 1969.* Vera Institute, New York, 1970.

Chapter 8

CORRECTIONS*

A s in the police and court settings, the human services move-ment is active in the correctional field as well. The thrust of nonprofessional programming in corrections primarily involves the following:

> 1. Upgrading the training and recognition of correction officers and the essential treatment roles they play in penal institutions.
> 2. Recruitment of minority group members.
> 3. Employment of ex-offenders.
> 4. Enlistment of a broad spectrum of volunteers.
> 5. Development of special training methods for nonpro-fessionals and volunteers.

After years of neglect, the problems of inappropriate person-nel utilization and ineffective manpower recruitment in correc-tions finally came to light with the publication of *A Time to Act* in 1969. The report was prepared by the Joint Commission on Correctional Manpower and Training and was the result of a study initiated in 1965 at the request of Congress. This report and the subsequent one, entitled *Corrections,* which was prepared by the National Advisory Commission on Criminal Justice Stand-ards and Goals, recognizes a long history of poor personnel man-agement and recommends significant changes in recruitment, training, and staff utilization policies.

These reports traced the personnel policies of various correc-tional agencies and found a basic lack in general strategy for future manpower development, the presence of low employment requirements, and an acceptance of the practice of political patronage as a means of filling correctional positions.

Along with the above findings, the National Advisory Com-

*See also Appendix 8.

124

mission report (1973) contains several other factors which complicate the hiring and utilization of personnel who would be in the best position to further the rehabilitation of offenders:

> Institutions were in isolated rural areas where it was difficult to induce professional staff to locate. Manpower was drawn largely from the local population and thus reflected a rural point of view out of line with that of most offenders, who came from the cities.
>
> Historically, corrections personnel resembled military and law enforcement officers. Correctional staff members were used almost entirely in paramilitary capacities, even in the State "Schools" for juveniles and youths. Parole officers were more akin to law enforcement officers than to "helping service" personnel . . .
>
> This identification with the military strongly influenced manpower and training policies and practices. Staff members were promoted up the ranks. They were not to fraternize with the inmates, who were to call them "sir." They conducted inspections and kept demerit lists. They were trained in military matters.
>
> In all too many modern correctional institutions, these policies and practices remain. Great conflict is evident as this militaristic system is confronted today by persons urging adoption of modern organizational concepts. (P. 465)

Accordingly, the need for improved and innovative staff recruitment, retention, and education programs is unquestionable today if we are to provide corrections with suitable personnel. Modern programs and philosophies cannot be actualized if outmoded, unresponsive personnel practices are to remain. Consequently, instead of administrators focusing their attention on filling the positions they now have in their table of organization, a bold move is necessary to examine the job descriptions they now have to see if they're still relevant. Once this is done, new positions should be added, inappropriate ones disregarded, and yet other ones redirected. Included in this last category should be the correctional line personnel, the ones who in the past were referred to as "guards" and are now technically designated as "correction officers."

THE NEW CORRECTION OFFICER

Old stereotypes are hard to change. Even though the title "Correction Officer" or "C.O." has been in use for some time, the line personnel in penal institutions are often still referred to as "guards" by the press and many university professors.

This mistake reflects a lack of appreciation of the many roles the modern correction officer fills. He/she may be a public relations representative, carpenter, halfway house director, librarian, program director, counselor; the skills and positions of today's correctional line personnel are often quite varied and sophisticated.

Today's correction officer does not just *guard* people, so the old term really is not applicable. While the new title of C.O. does still reflect the limited law enforcement-type caste, it is a move to give correctional personnel a level of status with the other criminal justice workers in the system.

> To the news media, the longtime "star" of the criminal justice system has been the law enforcement officer. When five city police officers and three federal agents join forces to surround and arrest a bank robber, it makes news.
>
> Yet, little credit is given to the lone, unarmed correction officer who is often locked in with this criminal and over 100 other such offenders, with only his personal and professional talents as his weapons. (Wicks 1974a, P. 32)

The C.O. has no choice. He must be able to function as a "practical psychologist"—even more so than his police counterpart on the street. To help him accomplish this, training must be provided in those areas of human behavior which can prove useful in his interactions with the population which far outnumber him when he is on the tier or in the institution's dayroom.

As well as knowing principles of crowd control and how to handle grievances, the C.O. should also be aware of psychological principles in order to help in the treatment of the inmate. Though it is the prison's mental health staff members who are trained to handle abnormal behavioral episodes, they are usually not present in the blocks or near the cells when something unusual occurs. For instance, if someone threatens suicide, it is the C.O., not the psychologist, who must act promptly to prevent unnecessary loss of life. Therefore, it is important that the C.O. receive training in the behavioral sciences in order to prevent unfortunate outcomes to psychological emergencies in the institution (Wicks 1972).

Likewise, due to understaffing in the rehabilitation staff and the institutional realities that dictate a situation where an inmate may only see a psychologist forty-five minutes each week, it would be prudent to train the C.O. as a "helping agent" since he is in almost constant contact with the offenders. If the C.O. sets a good role model and provides a healthy milieu in the living and work areas, he can have a good deal of impact. In the same vein, if he is brutal or ignorant of how he can assist the inmate to gain a foothold back in society, he can do enough harm to eliminate what positive impact any institutional program may have.

With this in mind, training and retraining programs for C.O.s as well as hiring procedures designed to attract treatment-oriented personnel have been instituted in some cities and states. In New York City, for example, the Center for Correctional Training developed a new curriculum which contains courses that are not directly concerned with inmate control or building security systems.

Some of the behaviorally oriented courses were applied psychology for correction officers, suicide prevention, and ethnic awareness. Also, the New York City Department of Correction conducted an in-service course which included both group work and didactic presentations. This program, conducted in conjunction with the National Urban League (NUL), was set up with the hope that it could sensitize the participants to the new inmate and alert them to the new correction officer roles as helper and leader, instead of guardian and controller.

In this training, one of the important objectives was to "train the trainers." In the early phases of the in-service training conducted by the N.Y.C. Department of Correction and the NUL, an effort was made to train correction officers to conduct the training. In this way, the training process could continue after the initial grant expired. Moreover, if correction officers conducted the training, they might have more credibility with the officers.

As well as the N.Y.C. Department of Correction's efforts to sensitize and resensitize their personnel generally to the needs and attitudes of the inmate population, some programs have recognized the logic of training C.O.s to be part of the treatment team. This is particularly pertinent in those settings which employ behavior modification techniques such as the "token economy."

In the token economy the person is given checks, chits, tokens, or some sort of physical notation if he behaves in accordance with specifically established norms. If he does not do what he is supposed to (clean living area, refrain from physical violence), he loses points or tokens. The reason why the tokens are important is that they can be exchanged in some settings for goods or privileges. In a prison this may mean that an inmate can earn cigarettes, more freedom while incarcerated, or actually an early release.

However, if a behavioral program is to be effective in jail, the C.O. must be included. Since he is in constant contact with the inmate, he will need to be aware of what behavior should be reinforced so that its frequency will increase in the inmate who connects his actions with the reward received. Likewise, he will need to understand the necessity to ignore inappropriate behavior as much as is realistically possible so that it will decrease and eventually disappear once it is no longer reinforced by attention. Essentially, the officer will have to see the institutional activities in a behavioral framework, or a behavior modification program will not be effective (Pooley 1969).

Though the human services movement in corrections includes this widespread support for providing correction officers with training and actual roles in the mental health field, there are naturally problems which are hampering such efforts. Some of them are due to personality factors in the officers themselves. Some officers are too rigid or resistant to accept new potential alternatives to handling people and situations. Others are fearful of moving out of a militaristic mold. Personality factors, however, are not the primary reason for failure in the move to assist correctional line personnel to serve as nonprofessional (or practical) psychologists. As was alluded to previously, the *system* itself is a problem.

When hiring new personnel, it is usually done under the impression that the new recruits are to function as criminal justice *officers*. Persons on civil service lists for correction officer are often also on lists to become police officers or sheriffs. In other words, as the city or state has it set up, people are being attracted to a C.O. position with the expectation of it being a police officer-type position.

The other side of this unfortunate coin is that, in reality, such a recruitment description is often accurate. In fact, because of a poor physical plant, the lack of programs, the incorrigibility of a portion of the population, and the demand for "security first!" by the public, C.O.s must indeed serve as criminal justice officers first, and as changing agents second. So, before the currently employed C.O. can reach out to the new challenging—and desperately *needed*—roles within the human services realm, much alteration will have to take place in the system itself.

INDIGENOUS PARAPROFESSIONALS IN CORRECTIONS

Racial strife, misunderstandings, a disproportionate number of minorities found in the ranks of corrections, and a general feeling of alienation among an inmate population that sees itself as a disenfranchised group of political prisoners have finally led correctional administrators and commissioners to the belief that hiring indigenous paraprofessionals is a good idea. One question that comes to mind now, considering the often heavily weighted minority group presence in the inmate population of many institutions, is, Why wasn't this situation recognized and acted upon sooner? Unfortunately, another question that follows upon the previous one is, Why hasn't the situation been significantly rectified by now?

The Joint Commission on Correctional Manpower and Training (1969) reported that of 111,000 correctional employees, only 8 percent were blacks, 4 percent Chicanos, and less than 1 percent American Indians, Orientals, or Puerto Ricans. They also noted that *all* correctional administrators in adult institutions were white.

The National Advisory Commission (1973) reports that while this has slightly changed, the number of blacks is still greatly disproportionate to the black inmate population. It is small wonder then that, in the light of this lack of progress, clear standards on recruitment of minority groups have been set forth (see Fig. 8-1). The Commission is no longer willing to accept reasons for this situation; they believe it can be rectified if enough effort and innovative approaches are employed.

Recruitment for Minority Groups: A Standard for Corrections*

Correctional agencies should take immediate, affirmative action to recruit and employ minority group individuals (black, Chicano, American Indian, Puerto Rican, and others) for all positions.

1. All job qualifications and hiring policies should be reexamined with the assistance of equal employment specialists from outside the hiring agency. All assumptions (implicit and explicit) in qualifications and policies should be reviewed for demonstrated relationship to successful job performance. Particular attention should be devoted to the meaning and relevance of such criteria as age, educational background, specified experience requirements, physical characteristics, prior criminal record or "good moral character" specifications, and "sensitive job" designations. All arbitrary obstacles to employment should be eliminated.

2. If examinations are deemed necessary, outside assistance should be enlisted to insure that all tests, written and oral, are related significantly to the work performed and are not culturally biased.

3. Training programs, more intensive and comprehensive than standard programs, should be designed to replace educational and previous experience requirements. Training programs should be concerned also with improving relationships among culturally diverse staff and clients.

4. Recruitment should involve a community relations effort in areas where the general population does not reflect the ethnic and cultural diversity of the correctional population. Agencies should develop suitable housing, transportation, education, and other arrangements for minority staff, where these factors are such as to discourage their recruitment.

Figure 8-1.

---

*Source: National Advisory Commission on Criminal Justice Standards and Goals: *Corrections*. U.S. Government Printing Office, Washington, D.C., 1973, p. 474.

Excuses often are given that qualified members of minority groups cannot be found. One State administrator for the Southwestern region told the press recently: "Of the 128 women inmates, 48 are black. There are no Negro matrons on the staff. We simply have no black applicants, or they didn't meet the qualifications." Such remarks no longer can go unchallenged. (National Advisory Commission 1973, P. 474)

USE OF NONPROFESSIONALS

As well as indigenous paraprofessionals, nonprofessionals who are not from a minority group are also now being employed in the correctional setting. They too are making an impact in that they are filling positions formerly reserved only for professionals (Wicks 1974b).

Their work as interviewers, counselors, and group leaders is evident in this nation and abroad. In the United States, for example, young high school graduates were serving as interviewers in the reception block in New York City's correctional system. They were responsible—after receiving a training program—to elicit information (previous offenses, suicidal attempts, current behavior) which would help the coordinator to decide where each inmate should be housed and what specific treatment he might immediately need.

In the Providence Youth Interviewers Project, youths worked as individual and group counselors with clients of the same age. This program seemingly illustrated that youths will often be more open with people of their own age more readily than with those they perceive to be part of the establishment (Progress for Providence 1966).

Overseas in Okinawa, Marine Corps sergeants who did not have a college degree were put into positions where they performed counseling and social work functions that were normally considered to be only within the purview of college level workers. While there is no formal study to support the effectiveness of their work, reports from on-the-scene observers were positive.

In another foreign experiment with paraprofessionals in group work, Danish nonprofessionals were given the opportunity to lead sessions with a minimum of supervision following an intensive training period. In this training they were given advance experience of the potential difficulties in leading a group. For example, they were put in situations where they were pressured by their peers and where they had to demonstrate how they would get others to take the lead. This was done so they could get the feeling of what it would be like to be a group leader so they could apply their skills when such classic situations arose (Feldman 1970).

Retaining Nonprofessionals

Whether the nonprofessionals were caucasian or from a minority group, one problem that uniformly crops up is attrition. Due to low salary, poor training, and/or the absence of real opportunity for advancement, many new careerists in corrections leave within a year for a better paying job or one with a greater future. In response there have been some efforts exerted to improve the design of the nonprofessional's career plan. This includes steps to offer more effective in-service training, financial support for educational pursuits on the college level, and the opening up of administrative and supervisory positions for personnel entering as paraprofessionals. The results of such moves hopefully will end in the retainment of more trained paraprofessionals—particularly those from minority groups.

Unfortunately, the move to build in career ladders for new careerists can lead to problems. One potential difficulty reported (Wicks 1976) is that if paraprofessionals are given the opportunity to become a member of the "system," they may also change and acclimate to it to the point that they will no longer be in an ideal position to identify and thus empathize with the population they were hired to work with in the prison. To remedy this, the continued use of terminal, short term positions, as well as the maintenance of a career ladder, are recommended. The author believes that this cadre of workers will be able to offer the inmates a good deal as direct service agents—especially under the supervision of nonprofessional indigenous workers who had previously served in counseling roles.

Thus, the author feels that while the development of a career ladder is a necessity, the use of the nonprofessional who is not being groomed to be part of the staff permanently will provide the institution with a life line with the inmates' street community, as it will provide the inmate with someone he can easily relate to in the prison.

Just as the seasoned black ex-offender who has been out of trouble for ten years has something unique to offer an inmate or probationer, so does the former offender who has been going "straight" for only a year. Just as the Puerto Rican who after six years in corrections has been promoted to principal mental health worker has much to offer the offenders he works with that is special, so too will the young Puerto Rican who has just graduated from high school and still lives in a ghetto area.

Consequently, to attract, hire, and use *only* those indigenous paraprofessionals who are expected and encouraged to become a part of the system on a long term basis may be a mistake . . . (Wicks 1976, pp. 676, 677)

EMPLOYMENT OF EX-OFFENDERS

For a long time, legal barriers and agency regulations prevented ex-offenders from filling positions in corrections. Now the National Advisory Commission on Criminal Justice Standards and Goals (1973) is recommending that quick action be taken to include ex-offenders in correctional roles (see Fig. 8-2).

Employment of Ex-Offenders: A Standard for Corrections*

Correctional agencies should take immediate and affirmative action to recruit and employ capable and qualified ex-offenders in correctional roles.

1. Policies and practices restricting the hiring of ex-offenders should be reviewed and, where found unreasonable, eliminated or changed.

2. Agencies not only should open their doors to the recruitment of ex-offenders but also should actively seek qualified applicants.

3. Training programs should be developed to prepare ex-offenders to work in various correctional positions, and career development should be extended to them so they can advance in the system.

Figure 8-2.

---

*Source: National Advisory Commission on Criminal Justice Standards and Goals: *Corrections.* U.S. Government Printing Office, Washington, D.C., 1973, p. 478.

Some professionals in the field have been extremely demonstrative about the inclusion of ex-offenders in corrections work. J. D. Grant (1968) in a paper on the new careers development project went so far as to note that "Evidence is now accumulating to the point where it can be considered a crime against the taxpayer not to develop strategies for the use of the offender as manpower in corrections and law enforcement programming" (p. 234).

Marie Buckley, another correctional program specialist, describes the successfully released offender as an "expert" and relates the use of ex-offenders in one particular project:

> Project Re-Entry is a program through which ex-offenders who have "made it" on the outside voluntarily return to the prison on a regular basis. Their aim is to use their experience and insights to help men about to be released prepare themselves for a variety of problems they will meet on the outside. (Buckley 1972, P. 24)

However, even though ex-offenders may have a knowledge of corrections and may be able to develop some rapport with members of an inmate population, naturally, every ex-offender does not qualify for work with offenders. One obviously is not an expert offender-counselor by virtue simply of one's past experience as an inmate.

There is no doubt that many ex-offenders do have an insight into the problems of the inmate that an outsider could not practically attain. The credibility factor they also add to treatment programs is another plus. One other important advantage of finding a qualified ex-offender is that this person can help in securing other useful former inmates for the project. This last function can be extremely critical since selection of the ex-offender needs to be done with a good deal of care, or the person may prove useless or even harmful to the program.

The criteria used for hiring ex-offenders for any criminal justice-related position is better when it is explicit (see Fig. 8-3). Many things could go wrong if the person turns out to be either too pro— or anti-establishment.

Criteria and Rating Scale for Hiring Offenders*

1. The criteria used by the Boston Court Resource Project for hiring ex-offenders for advocate positions in a pretrial intervention project was:
   (a) A man who had served time in prison and who had been out of prison for at least a year.
   (b) One who had demonstrated responsibility in previous job(s).
   (c) An above-average intelligence.
   (d) An ability to establish rapport with varying types of people easily. This would include a flexibility of approach, warmth, and sensitivity.)
   (e) A strong commitment to human services with some related work experience.
   (f) No recent (two years) drug history.
   (g) Demonstrated responsibility in financial obligations and stable personal life.
   (h) Ability to articulate, and sufficient education (or equivalent) to do narrative reporting.
   (i) History of personal counseling and a positive attitude toward treatment methods and toward professionals.
   (j) Freedom from prejudices and judgmental attitudes.
   (k) Maturity, good judgment, and self-awareness.

2. Based upon the criteria shown above a rating scale was devised with adjectival and numerical values. The applicant was rated in each area and points given were summed. The minimum acceptable level was +15 points. The "gut reaction" of the interviewers to the applicant also carried some weight that was not qualified but could overrule the scale results. The rating scale was as follows:

Age	24–32	$+\frac{1}{2}$ pt.		Over 0 pt.
Health	Good	$+1$		Poor -1
Education (Reporting)	Good	$+\frac{1}{2}$	Fair $+\frac{1}{2}$	Poor -1
Family life	Good	$+2$	Fair $+1$	Poor -1
Finances (Mgr. Responsibility)	Good	$+1$		Poor -1
Has Auto	Yes	$+1$		No $\quad0$
Drug History	Over 2 yrs.	$+0$	Only 1 yr. -1	Under 1 yr. -3
Personal Habits	Good	$+1$	Fair $+\frac{1}{2}$	Poor -1
Work History	Good	$+1\frac{1}{2}$	Fair $+\frac{1}{2}$	Poor -0
Prejudices (Race, Judicial)	Yes	-2	Fair $-1\frac{1}{2}$	Poor $-\frac{1}{2}$

Flexibility	Good	$+1\frac{1}{2}$	Fair	$+\frac{1}{2}$	Poor	$-1\frac{1}{2}$
Attitude regarding system	Healthy	$+\frac{1}{2}$	Fair	$+\frac{1}{2}$	Poor	$-1\frac{1}{2}$
"Warmth"	Good	$+2$	Fair	$+1$	Poor	-2
Ability to articulate	Good	$+2$	Fair	$+1$	Poor	-2
Commitment	Good	$+3$	Fair	$+1\frac{1}{2}$	Poor	-1

Figure 8-3.

*Source: Boston Court Resource Project: Appendix. In McCreary, Phyllis Groom and McCreary, John M.: *Job Training and Placement for Offenders and Ex-Offenders.* U.S. Department of Justice, U.S. Government Printing Office, 1975.

It is easy for the ex-offender to be caught in between the pressures from the system on the one hand and the attraction of the commonality he has with the population on the other. When this occurs, even the most mature worker can become drawn into either extreme. In such a case there may be a desire to reject any identification with the offender population. In this instance, the price in terms of the ex-offender's usefulness is high, since the very reason he was hired was to provide a link between the clients and the staff. In distancing himself from them, he is counteracting the very reason and value of his initial employment.

The other danger is that the ex-offender would opt for joining in with the inmates in a fight against "the man," "the establishment," or the program. In doing this the worker is involved in complaining with the inmate and planning with him how to exploit rather than benefit from the program.

To prevent such occurrences from happening, the most useful techniques are good screening procedures, meaningful training, and continued group meetings to discuss difficulties that might be developing. In the training, the ex-offender's unique insights should be elicited and reinforced by their acceptance by the professionals. Instead of trying to change the former inmate into a "carbon copy professional," the training should concentrate on how to enhance the personal and job-related skills he already possesses.

The goal is to provide skills and on-the-job exposure to areas not particularly familiar to the ex-offender. Paper work, methods in work organization, and techniques in counseling are among the areas which need to be stressed in many instances (McCreary and

McCreary 1975). Even in the teaching of counseling skills, the goal is to provide the ex-offender with a framework to employ his own personality and background. It is not a "white people's" substitute. The idea is not to replace or remove the worker's unique talents and potential contributions, but to enhance and supplement them. With support, an understanding of personal discipline, and a working knowledge of the system, its paperwork, and operations, the ex-offender can be a key member in the overall treatment team.

Without proper training and a continued opportunity to express problems and seek advancement, poor performance should be expected. Lateness, inattention to work, or an alliance with the unhealthy aspects of the inmate population are among the negative results which may occur. When a program is run on the premise that its personnel will generally be present and achievement-oriented, habitual lateness and inattention to duty can be fatal to the program and to the section of the project dealing with screening, hiring, and training ex-offenders.

VOLUNTEERS IN CORRECTIONS

Just as there has been a recent push to recruit minority group members, nonprofessionals, and ex-offenders, there has also been a move to increase the participation of volunteers in corrections (see Fig. 8-4). The use of volunteers is not new. We have just gotten away from employing them in the most optimal ways possible.

Employment of Volunteers: A Standard for Corrections*

Correctional agencies immediately should begin to recruit and use volunteers from all ranks of life as a valuable additional resource in correctional programs and operations, as follows:

1. Volunteers should be recruited from the ranks of minority groups, the poor, inner-city residents, ex-offenders who can serve as success models, and professionals who can bring special expertise to the field.

2. Training should be provided volunteers to give them an under-

standing of the needs and lifestyles common among offenders and to acquaint them with the objectives and problems of corrections.

3. A paid volunteer coordinator should be provided for efficient program operation.

4. Administrators should plan for and bring about full participation of volunteers in their programs; volunteers should be included in organizational development efforts.

5. Insurance plans should be available to protect the volunteer from any mishaps experienced during participation in the program.

6. Monitary rewards and honorary recognition should be given to volunteers making exceptional contribution to an agency.

Figure 8-4.

*Source: National Advisory Commission on Criminal Justice Standards and Goals: *Corrections.* U.S. Government Printing Office, Washington, D.C., 1973, p. 480.

The National Advisory Commission notes that "In programs where volunteers have been used, paid employees feel that they have made a significant contribution and would like to see more of them. Where volunteers have not been used, employees are far from enthusiastic about starting to use them (p. 480). The correctional institution is traditionally a closed community. Not only do they not want the inmates to escape, they often do not want the community to get in. Such suspiciousness is particularly evident at the local level.

In many local jails and municipal institutions the only representation from the community is a group of volunteers who hand out religious magazines. Though such work is fine, it needs to be supplemented and expanded today. To achieve this, a number of organizations and commissions have provided information on volunteer utilization. These include:

- *Guidelines and Standards for the Use of Volunteers in Correctional Programs* (U.S. Department of Justice LEAA, Technical Assistance Division, Washington, D.C., 1972).
- *OAR* (Offender Aid and Restoration Group) *Volunteer's Book* (OAR, 414 4th Street N.E., Charlottesville, Va. 22901).

With a vigorous recruitment, training, and retraining program, a volunteer program can be creatively developed. By attracting minority group members, professionals from varied fields, and increasing the present traditional volunteer's awareness of the lifestyle of the modern inmate, the volunteer force can become a major link between the inmate and the free community.

Final Comments

Human services in the correctional field centers on the modernization of the correction officer's (C.O.'s) role and the establishment of a new career ladder for paraprofessionals. In this respect, it has met with some degree of success, but as in other quarters it has had its share of problems, too.

Some correctional officers have rejected roles for themselves outside of those involving strictly security-police functions. Certain systems have also had a place in blocking the progressive development of the C.O.'s role. While the officers have been ready to move into new roles, certain departments of correction have been unwilling to provide the training and opportunities for them to move into paralegal and practical psychology roles.

The other major aspect of correctional human services—the new careers movement—has met with some resistance from administrative and line personnel as well. The idea of letting ex-offenders and untrained nonprofessionals actually work in the prison as staff members was just too radical an idea for some. They felt using people who had a record or those who did not qualify as a "legitimate professional" should not be permitted into the institution. The fear was that such personnel might be subversive and align with the prisoners against the staff.

Some correctional planners and administrators have taken the chance though. They have even used paraprofessionals who were being maintained on methadone to work in drug programs and have allowed ex-felons who have done well to work as counselors. *The results of such experiments are questionable, but the necessity of undertaking them are not.*

Corrections in its present state is *not* working! Past staff definitions have proved inadequate. Consequently, unless we attempt to seek further human resources, we can expect more of the same—more *failure*—and this is unacceptable!

REFERENCES

Buckley, Marie: Enter: the ex-con. *Federal Probation, 36*(4), 1972.

Feldman, Wulff: Group counseling in Danish prisons. *Police, 15*(1), 40-44, 1970.

Grant, J. D.: The offender as a correctional manpower resource. In Reissman, Frank and Popper, Hermine I. (Eds.): *Up From Poverty: New Career Ladders for Nonprofessionals.* Harper & Row, New York, 1968.

Joint Commission on Correctional Manpower and Training: *A Time To Act.* U.S. Government Printing Office, 1969.

McCreary, Phyllis Groom and McCreary, John M.: *Job Training and Placement for Offenders and Ex-Offenders.* U.S. Department of Justice, U.S. Government Printing Office, 1975.

National Advisory Commission on Criminal Justice Standards and Goals: *Corrections.* U.S. Department of Justice, U.S. Government Printing Office, Washington, D.C., 1973.

Pooley, Richard C.: *The Control of Human Behavior in a Correctional Setting.* Center for the Study of Crime and Delinquency, Carbondale, Illinois, 1969.

Progress for Providence: *Laying It on the Line . . . A Report on the Providence Youth Interviews Project.* Providence, Rhode Island, 1966.

Wicks, Robert J.: Indigenous correctional paraprofessionals: "bourgeois nigger or empathetic worker?" A brief position paper. *Journal of Sociology and Social Welfare, 3*(6), 672-78, 1976.

———: Is the correctional officer a second class citizen? *American Journal of Correction, 36*(1), 32, 34, 1974a.

———: *Correctional Psychology.* Canfield Press/Harper & Row, San Francisco, 1974b.

———: Suicide prevention: a guide for correction officers. *Federal Probation, 36*(3), 29-30, 1972.

Chapter 9

EDUCATION

AMERICAN SCHOOLS and the systems they carefully fit within
have traditionally been extremely rigid and stratified. As
recently as the 1950s most of the nation's primary and secondary
schools were "ivory tower institutions" quite divorced from the
community and the inner problems which were beginning to
beset them.

Finally in the 1960s the bubble burst. People began to voice
their dissatisfaction with a school system that no longer—or for
that matter, for a long time had not—met the needs of their community. The people wanted their schools back. They wanted
education to be relevant, equal, and related to the lives of the
locale and the family. The feeling was in many communities that
schools were becoming too distant, and parent-teacher associations
were not effective enough.

While this was occurring, the time was becoming ripe to open
the schools to the new careers movement. Teachers were over-
burdened with work, some of it quite irrelevant. School systems'
budgets were straining and large classes were being deemed part
of the answer. To deal with these problems, systems started to
experiment with the use of paraprofessionals. Workers such as
these would not only stretch the school system's dollar, but would
also relieve the teachers of inappropriate and excessive additional
opportunities. In addition, by recruiting people for these jobs
from the school's neighborhood, the link to the community could
be made stronger. Then, instead of having the school move
further away from the life line of the area, which would only
serve to increase animosity between the teaching professionals and
the people, the community could be effectively involved in the
activity of the school in a meaningful way.

IMPETUS FOR CHANGE

The dissatisfaction of numerous community leaders with the educational status quo that had been perpetuated for years by school professionals and the inability of teachers to meet the increasing needs of the large numbers of new students were behind the move to change educational services. However, there were other factors that also proved to be crucial in motivating structural change in education (Bowman and Klopf 1968).

One of these factors was the recognition that modern education needed teachers to be in a position to fill specialized, complex roles. Also, the usually middle-class teacher required assistance from someone atune to the community so that special needs of minority groups and those classifiable as "socioeconomically deprived" might not be left with their unique needs unmet.

The federal government also had a hand in the impetus for change in education. They provided funds to recruit, train, and utilize new personnel from the ranks of the poor and educationally unadvanced. Through the Office of Economic Opportunity, the Javits-Kennedy Act for Impacted Areas, and other federal acts, new, significant funding opened up and encouraged the establishment of new careers and opportunities to move from entry positions to jobs within the established ranks (see Table 9-I). Led by the funding and prompted by the other factors, school systems began contemplating new career ladders. One example of this was the large New York City system.

Career Ladder Concept in New York City
Board of Education

The human services movement's support of paraprofessional utilization as a means of dealing with the current staffing shortages in various fields was reflected in the New York City Board of Education's establishment of a new section called the Auxiliary Educational Career Unit (AECU). The AECU was created within the Board's department of personnel to administer the Educational Careers Program. This program began in the fall of 1967 and was to involve colleges from the area and the city's Human Resources Administration.

TABLE 9-I
POSSIBLE STAGES IN CAREER DEVELOPMENT OF AUXILIARIES*

1) AIDE SUCH AS	*Illustrative Functions*	*Training Suggested*
GENERAL SCHOOL AIDE ...	Clerical, monitorial custodial duties	Brief orientation period (2 or 3 weeks) in human development, social relations, and the school's goals and procedures, as well as some basic skill training.
LUNCHROOM AIDE	Serving and preparation of food, monitorial duties	
TEACHER AIDE	Helping teacher in classroom, as needed	
FAMILY WORKER OR AIDE .	Appointments, escorting, and related duties	
COUNSELOR AIDE	Clerical, receptionist, and related duties	no specified preschooling required.
LIBRARY AIDE	Helping with cataloging and distribution of books	

2) ASSISTANT SUCH AS	*Illustrative Functions*	*Training Suggested*
TEACHER ASSISTANT	More relationship to instructional process	High school diploma or equivalent; one year's in-service training or one year in college with practicum.
FAMILY ASSISTANT	Home visits and organizing parent meetings	
COUNSELOR ASSISTANT	More work with records, listening to children sent from class to counselor's office because they are disrupting class	both can be on a work-study basis while working as an aide.
LIBRARY ASSISTANT	More work with pupils in selecting books and reading to them	

3) ASSOCIATE SUCH AS	*Illustrative Functions*	*Training Suggested*
TEACHER ASSOCIATE	More responsibility with less supervision by the professional	A.A. degree from two-year college or two-year special program in a four-year college.
HOME-SCHOOL ASSOCIATE .		
COUNSELOR ASSOCIATE ...		
LIBRARY ASSOCIATE		
SOCIAL WORK ASSOCIATE ..		both can be on work-study basis while working as an assistant.

4) TEACHER - INTERN SUCH AS	*Illustrative Functions*	*Training Suggested*
STUDENT TEACHER	Duties very similar to those of associate but with more involvement in diagnosis and planning	B.A. or B.S. degree and enrollment in a college of teacher education or other institution which offers a program leading to certification.
STUDENT HOME-SCHOOL COORDINATOR		
STUDENT COUNSELOR		

5) TEACHER

*Source: Bowman, Garda W., Klopf, Gordon J., et al.: *Final Report of a Study for the Office of Economic Opportunity: New Careers and Roles in the American School.* Bank Street College of Education, New York, 1968, p. 21.

The program was designed initially to achieve a number of objectives in line with most projects of this type in the educational field. However, among the goals, two seemed to stand out. One was to improve the quality of education in certain sections of the city where poverty was a glaring reality. The other was to create a career ladder for entering paraprofessionals (see Table 9-II).

TABLE 9-II

BOARD OF EDUCATION OF THE CITY OF NEW YORK
AUXILIARY EDUCATIONAL CAREER UNIT*
THE CAREER LADDER CONCEPT

Title–Salary	Qualifications	Training	Job Description
†APPRENTICE-INTERN-TEACHER	3 yrs. college 2 semesters as Educational Assistant	Auxiliary Personnel	Assists in instruction of assigned class
†EDUCATIONAL ASSOCIATE	2 yrs. college (60 Credits) 2 semesters as an Educational Assistant	in all positions on The Career Ladder	Assumes increasing responsibilities with minimal direction from the teacher
EDUCATIONAL ASSISTANT $2.50 per hour $2.25 per hour	60 college credits High School Diploma or Equivalency Diploma	receive initial on-going in-service	Assists classroom teacher with monitorial, clerical and instructional tasks
EDUCATIONAL TRAINEE Stipend by funding agencies	Minimum-equivalent of 8th grade education	training	Assists with monitorial and clerical tasks

*Source: Bowman, Garda W., Klopf, Gordon J., et al.: *Final Report of a Study for the Office of Economic Opportunity: New Careers and Roles in the American School.* Bank Street College of Education, New York, 1968, p. 214.

†Project titles, not yet approved, and not designed to go into the Civil Service classification, but rather into the Pedagogical classification.

In the first two years of operation this program certainly moved into action quickly to get the new personnel selected, involved, and trained. In September of 1968, the beginning of their second year, 2,000 professionals and paraprofessionals had received training related to the program, 3,000 educational assistant positions had been created, and close to 900 assistants were enrolled in the City University of New York at several of their colleges. Close attention was paid to this program because—outside of the increased activism of the community boards—the birth of a new educational position with an impact comparable to that of the teacher was having a profound effect on modern education. The position being referred to is the "teacher aide."

TEACHER AIDE

If one takes the time to review the history and current uses of the teacher aide position, one point becomes quite evident. This new auxiliary teacher role is essential to the progressive advancement of modern education. From whatever view one takes, the teacher aide position appears valuable.

From the teacher's standpoint, the teacher aide (TA) is an uncertified staff member who serves as an assistant in a wide range of activities and responsibilities (see Fig. 9-1). These TA roles depend on the latitude given by the individual school system, teacher, and principal.

Teacher Aide Functions and Titles: A Sample

Monitorial duties
Clerical work
Audio-visual technician
Musician for class
Crisis intervention aide
Playground supervisor
Material preparation
Stockroom supervisor
Hallway supervisor
Assistant librarian
Homemaking aide
Science lab assistant
Testing monitor

Recreational assistant
Attendance & Homework evaluator
Transportation coordinator
Reading skills supervisor
Community activities coordinator

Figure 9-1.

If the auxiliary teacher program is rigidly stratified with the entry position listed at TA, the duties may be restricted simply to mechanical activities involving only clerical-monitorial duties. But in this case the TA is given the opportunity to move up the career ladder to the point of reaching the title of "teacher" (see Table 9-I).

In many systems, though, the assignments given to the TA vary in responsibility and complexity. It is the teacher and principal who decide how much authority and pupil involvement will be permitted. The decision in this instance is made according to the individual abilities of the particular TA and the flexibility of the school professionals involved. This approach is in direct contrast to the specifically structured one briefly discussed above.

In the structured system, the duties are carefully limited. This can be seen in the following quote from *The Teacher Aide in the Instructional Team,* which was prepared by Don Welty, Director of Education, College of the Desert, and Dorothy Welty, Elementary Teacher, Rancho Mirage Elementary School (1976):

[The] tasks for which an aide is *not* responsible . . . are:
1. Organization of curriculum.
2. Evaluation of the students.
3. Deciding on educational materials and methods to be used.
4. Subjective entries in pupil records.
5. Developing evaluative intruments.
6. Conferring with parents.
7. Referring students for special help or assignments.
8. Making lesson plans.
9. Deciding on discipline methods.
10. Setting classroom policy.
11. Counseling students in their educational plans.   (Italics supplied) (p. 16).

Whatever the role of the TA, the benefit to the teacher and to the pupils is potentially high. With increased staffing and a decreased teaching personnel-student ratio, much more can be accomplished in the classroom. Students can receive more individualized attention, and the structure necessary in larger classes with one teacher can be relaxed enough to permit more creative, small group activities.

TA and the Community

Particularly when the school system establishes a new careers program and seeks people from the local area to fill entry positions, a number of positive elements can come out of the TA program. Obviously, the issue of paid employment is one of the benefits of recruiting, training, and utilizing indigenous personnel. In addition, the community becomes more involved in the day-to-day operation of the school on the staff level, community students have someone from their neighborhood with whom they can readily identify, and the school administrator has a staff member who can help explain to the community board the unique workings and problems in operating the school.

History

The use of TAs largely began in the 1960s, but the rationale behind the use of educational assistants was tested as early as the 1950s. The three experiments that stood out took place in New Jersey, Michigan, and Connecticut (Ford Foundation 1961).

A primary result of these projects, unfortunately, was not positive. Their initiation brought about a negative reaction from teachers who saw the funding of these experiments as an undercutting of teacher job expansion. There was an expression of anger that the money allotted to the programs was not funnelled into hiring additional professional personnel.

The main breakthrough, however, was with the passing of the Elementary and Secondary Education Act of 1965 (Title I) and the Education Professions Development Act. These acts, as well as the ones cited in the beginning of the chapter, supported upgrading low-income area schools, partly through the use of indigenous personnel in new professions.

Since these acts of the mid-1960s, many approaches have been taken by school systems throughout America. (For an elucidation of seven extensive programs, see the *Final Report* of a study conducted by Bank Street College of Education for the Office of Economic Opportunity; the full reference is listed at the end of the chapter.) Presently, the new careers movement—particularly in low-income, urban settings—is deeply entrenched in the nation's educational structure.

Recruitment

Attracting appropriate candidates for teacher aide positions is not a simple pursuit for school systems. In many cases, to qualify for federal funding under Title I of the Elementary and Secondary Education Act of 1965, efforts must be directed at obtaining TA trainees from low-income areas.

The way this might be accomplished is by the school system contacting community organizations and letting them know of their needs regarding TAs. Once the TA program is in operation, existing aides can also serve as informal recruiters. There are other ways and agencies that can also be tapped.

> In Maine, mothers receiving Aid to Dependent Children were informed of the program by their social workers. The Navaho auxiliaries in Northern Arizona were recruited through the Bureau of Indian Affairs, radio announcements, and word-of-mouth publicity on the reservation. The availability of programs at Ohio and in Puerto Rico was made known to classes of local high schools by the principals or guidance counselors. Mass media were used in almost every project to supplement other forms of recruitment. (Bowman and Klopf 1968, P. 27)

Selection

As one can imagine, the selection criteria—because of the variance in job functions among and within different school systems—was not uniform for all TA programs. The following are some of the criteria used to screen new applicants (no school system used all of these factors, but most sought people who had several of these qualities or educational talents) :

1. Motivation and enthusiasm to work with students.

2. High school diploma.

3. Resident of low-income area.

4. Unemployed.

5. Previous history of employment in schools in some capacity.

6. Personableness and general ability to work with others.

7. Member of certain minority group which was in the majority in the school to which the particular TA was to be assigned.

8. Possessed talent in specific mechanical area, i.e. audio-visual aide, homemaking aide.

9. Had no schooling beyond sixth grade.

10. Possessed a two-year/four-year degree in education.

As can be plainly seen, some of the above requirements are on opposite ends of the pole. Some programs were looking for entry workers in a new careers program and sought people with a high school diploma, currently unemployed, from a certain low-income area, who showed an aptitude for advancement up the ladder to teacher. Other programs had very few or no real requirements beyond acceptable physical and mental health. Yet others viewed their auxiliary personnel as teacher associates and expected them to have college degrees, with certification being the only factor differentiating them from the teacher.

Training

The variance among teacher aide programs continues even through the training procedures. The pre-service and on-the-job training was geared to the roles of the TAs. In those positions where the responsibilities of the TA were quite similar to the teacher's, the prerequisite education was a four-year degree in education or a two-year course specifically designed for the future teacher aide (see Fig. 9-2).

FIRST YEAR

First Semester		Credits
361	English Composition I (3;0)	3
810	Basic Psychology (3;0)	3
840	Introduction to Sociology (3;0)	3
530	History I Elective (3;0) [530 or 531]	3
	Mathematics Elective (3;0) [681 or 683]	3
	Physical Education Elective (0;2)	1
		16

Second Semester		
362	English Composition II (3;0)	3
812	Psychology of Adjustment (3;0)	3
842	Social Problems (3;0)	3
532	History II Elective (3;0) [532 or 533]	3
	Science Elective (3;0) or (2;4) [130 or 180]	3 or 4
	Physical Education Elective (0;2)	1
		16 or 17

SECOND YEAR

First Semester		
	Social Science Electives (3;0) (3;0)	3 and 3
	Psychology Elective (3;0)	3
	Liberal Arts Elective (3;0)	3
	Science Elective (3;0) or (2;4) [131 or 182]	3 or 4
571	Critical Analysis and Problems in Health (1;0)	1
		16 or 17

Second Semester		
943	Supervised Practicum and Seminar (2;8) *or*	
932	Practicum in Instructional Methodology (2;8) or [813 and 717]	6
787	Metropolitan Government (3;0)	3
934	Introduction to Counseling and Guidance (3;0)	3
936	Classroom Management (3;0) *or*	
844	Introduction to Human Services (3;0) *or*	
	Liberal Arts Elective (3;0)	3
		15

Figure 9-2. Human Services Curriculum, Teacher Aide Option, for Camden County College, Blackwood, New Jersey: This program prepares students to become teacher aides in public and private schools. Source: Camden County College *Bulletin* 1975–1976.

In the in-service courses the curriculum varied, depending up-on the specific tasks to be performed by the often specialized role of the TAs in question. Usually, however, there was basic in-formation on the structure and function of the individual school and system. In addition, there was information disseminated in lectures, small groups, and through audio-visual means on de-velopmental psychology, educational philosophy, crisis interven-tion, and working as a team member.

Under the rubric of in-service training was the TA super-vision received from the teacher and other members of the profes-sional staff. This section of the training was most important since TAs were so different in their backgrounds and previous educa-tion; they required individualized attention if their potential tal-ents were to be further developed within the context of the educa-tional system.

Problems and Conflicts in Utilizing TAs

Any new program, no matter the extent or organization it is developed within, is bound to come up against initial problems and conflicts at each level of responsibility and authority. Initial teacher aide programs were no exception to this course of events—particularly in its early stages.

For the *superintendent,* the key difficulties involved admini-strative red tape in setting up the staffing and fiscal structure for the new position, or career ladder. Convincing and supervising each principal to see the value of using paraprofessionals was also in some cases a real chore.

Once the *principals* realized that the teacher aide position was going to be a reality, they had to set up a structure and climate in which the TA would be able to receive training and operate successfully. This meant not only ensuring that schedules re-flected time and staffing for training, supervision, and optimal utilization of the TAs, but also it created a need for the principal to explain the program in such a way that the teachers would not feel too threatened, confused, or put upon by the program.

The *teachers* frequently became alarmed that their jobs would be supplanted by incoming, lower-salaried paraprofessionals.

(This is a normal fear held by professionals during the initial phase of a new careers project in any of the human services.) They also were concerned about how they would interact with the TAs and provide guidance for them. Previously, they just had to be responsible for their classes, which were normally held without the presence of another adult. Now they would be required to share their responsibilities with another person and be subject during the day to the TA's possibly "watchful eye."

Teacher aides, on the other hand, were also full of conflict about this new role for them. How would they be accepted? Could they do their job? Would the training be too difficult for them? Would they be as uncomfortable in this system as they had been in other ones in the past?

Parents experienced problems, too, over the use of TAs. While they were generally pleased with the addition of new staff, some had a nagging fear that a program such as this might lead to lower educational standards because of the paraprofessional personnel involved, rather than raising them because of the lower staff-student ratio.

No one was spared having at least some anguish in the move to add new types of personnel to the existing educational staff. In certain instances, where the school's staff was not prepared for the TA's entry into their system, hostility, confusion, and even overt teacher resistance in the classroom setting resulted.

Conflicts between teachers and the new TAs, failure to provide time for TA training on the part of the principal, and TA defensiveness to the point of undercutting class discipline and educational progress were unfortunate results in those instances where the system's schools were not set up to deal with a new paraprofessional program. Not every system or school had great difficulties, though. Ones who took the time to prepare new and existing staff obviously had the least amount of problems.

Educational planners who sought to delineate TA roles and establish orientation for new TAs and current professionals as to the teamwork concept and the mutual values to be gotten out of the program were rewarded with less teacher and assistant backlash. Communication facilitation groups (small groups in which teachers are asked to interact with a leader concerning the use of TAs), supervision for teachers in their new roles as TA supervisors, creative training for new TAs, and time and administrative support for continuous training for *both* teachers and TAs are among the positive steps taken by most systems to deal with the influx of new careerists.

Figure 9-3. A teacher's assistant instructing a class. (Photo courtesy of Parkway Day School, Germantown, Pennsylvania.)

Final Comments

Of all the settings where new professionals have been employed, the educational environment was one of the most logical and appropriate ones. The certified personnel, i.e. teachers and principals, needed assistance as the link between the institution (school) and the community was becoming tenuous by the beginning of the era of the new careerist movement (1950s and 1960s).

The ready availability of federal funds for education was a primary impetus for the teacher aide program. However, the notable factor in the use of auxiliary personnel in education is that, even granting the availability of such funds, the educational programs as a whole have produced a better implementation of new careers programs than many others in the human services settings who also have received funding.

REFERENCES

Bowman, Garda W., Klopf, Gordon J., et al.: *Final Report of a Study for the Office of Economic Opportunity: New Careers and Roles in the American School.* Bank Street College of Education, New York, 1968.

Ford Foundation, The Fund for the Advancement of Education: *Decade of Experiment: 1951-1961,* 1961.

Welty, Don A. and Welty, Dorothy R.: *The Teacher Aide in the Institutional Team.* McGraw-Hill, New York, 1976.

Chapter 10

SOCIAL WORK

A SOCIAL ASSISTANCE agency in a position to offer a myriad of services, via different types of helping agents, would be likely to have a potentially positive impact on the community it is set up to serve. To be such an ideal organization, the agency would need to be able to efficiently utilize professional social workers (M.S.W.—Master's degree in social work) and case workers (B.A./B.S.W.), as well as an entire spectrum of differently talented nonprofessional technicians.

Without such a team of helping agents, some people in the community might not seek help. Other would-be clients would have to wait long. Still others might feel put off or misunderstood by a social worker (as opposed to an indigenous nonprofessional) and leave the agency in a frame of mind so negative that they would then dissuade others from seeking help there. Social work agencies need to utilize a team approach if they are to attract people in need and be able to successfully treat them.

Clients have different needs and come from varied backgrounds. As in any mental health pursuit, it is always advantageous if the treatment and treatment agent can be matched to the client. Some people need to be seen by a professional social worker; either the professional's expertise is required, or the client in question is unable to relate to a nonprofessional. However, in many cases, the opposite situation exists; the potential client would not come to the agency if an outreach worker from the community did not urge him or her to do so. Then when this person did come, such a client might well also only accede to treatment if it would be undertaken by an indigenous paraprofessional —someone from the client's neighborhood and background to whom he could relate during this crisis.

Yet, stating that social agencies need to utilize a team approach is almost passé now. Of course, casework organizations should use professionals and nonprofessionals together—they have done it for years. The question is, *how* are nonprofessionals to be employed, and where do the professional workers fit into the team schema?

As Alex Rosen in his paper (1960) on the shortage of professional personnel correctly notes, "How much the expert accomplishes is partly determined by the number and skill of his assistants and how he uses them" (p. 72). One might naturally include under the heading of "assistants" not only nonprofessionals and indigenous paraprofessionals in particular, but also volunteers.

VOLUNTEERS

The volunteer movement is as active in social work as it is in any aspect of the human services movement in general. Nonsalaried personnel have been called upon to function in a variety of settings with both children and adults. In addition, the volunteers used have come from the ranks of business, government, and different allied professions. One of the unique aspects of the volunteer programs in social work, though, is the willingness of project directors to successfully employ housewives, teenagers, and other potential helpers in service roles normally not considered within their abilities by non-social work agencies. Possibly because of social work's continual use of nonprofessional positions and the fact that it grew out of an understanding of the value of community spirit and helping one's neighbor, social workers have been more willing to experiment with the use of volunteers. Whatever the reason, however, some of their experiments with generally untrained persons are as practical and successful as they are bold.

Housewives as Case Aides

In 1965, a special pilot study was set up at the Metropolitan State Hospital in Waltham, Massachusetts. In this pilot project "mature" housewives were recruited to work as volunteer case aides.

Recruiting was done through the newspapers and via informal meetings. Each of the women was screened in an interview. The make-up of the group varied, though there were some commonalities.

> The twenty-five women who participated in the project ranged from twenty-five to fifty-five, the majority being in their thirties or early forties. All had at least one child, of school age or younger. Most of the women had been previously involved in community activities, for the most part in church work, or scouting. Sixteen of the twenty-five had had personal therapy of some kind or had first-hand knowledge of mental illness, either through a close relative or through previous employment; none had been mentally ill.

> Thirteen of the case aides were college graduates, and six more had attended college though they had not completed their courses; the remaining six were high school graduates. Their husbands' occupations were for the most part professional; eight were in skilled technical work or business enterprises. (Cain and Epstein 1967, P. 282).

Training was carried out through group meetings, personal supervision, and lecture groups. Each phase of the educational program was set up to help the women deal more effectively on a one-to-one basis with the female clients they had.

One of the ways the professional social workers dealt with the volunteers' possible misconceptions regarding the population they were working with was to keep from them all data on their clients, except for their identifying data. The extensive historical data on the clients which was contained in the records was given to the volunteers after they had had a chance to meet with their clients for several sessions. This approach also proved to be a motivating factor for the volunteer to get acquainted with her client as soon as possible (Cain and Epstein 1967, p. 283).

The population which the volunteers served was not an easy one. Many of the clients had been diagnosed as "schizophrenic," and some of them had been hospitalized for as much as thirty years. However, even though this was the case, Lillian Cain and Doris Epstein reported that "mature housewives—though initially untrained—possess common sense, imagination, experience, and empathy that can be of significant help to the mentally ill" (p. 284).

Though these investigators felt that one of the important outcomes of the study was to show that "housewives" could help solve the personnel shortage in social work agencies, a broader issue appears at stake here, namely, the fact that society's discrimination against the nonprofessional woman has kept us from benefitting from the potential she brings as a person to the human services area.

Casting the noncareer women as a "housewife" who possesses merely routine homemaking skills is just as bad—and inaccurate—as casting a minority group member as incapable of serving social service functions simply because this individual has not received formal training up to this point. The agency which has been willing to open its doors to volunteers and to develop a basic training program has found out that the volunteer can not only perform professional activities in many cases, but also this type of worker can often add a new dimension to the treatment approach as well.

Volunteer Work with Children

In a possibly more traditional, but no less important, program than the one with noncareer women, Irvin Kraft (1966) reports on the use of volunteers as social work technicians in a child psychiatry clinic. The impetus for the development of it, however, is a bit more mundane.

> To eliminate procedures (such as taking the usual detailed social history) that did not seem to contribute appreciably to the psychiatric resident's learning process, we thought of utilizing social-work technicians; but none was available. We had no funds for training them. Faced with these facts, we began, six years ago, to train volunteers for technical tasks that could be splintered off from the duties of the child psychiatrist, the psychiatric social worker, and the clinical psychologist. (Kraft 1965, p. 460)

Unlike many volunteer programs, this one had no formal recruitment or screening process. The program expanded primarily through people finding out about it through word of mouth and then deciding to become involved. The training program was likewise not very structured but was rather casual and mainly directed at helping the volunteer become accustomed to the jargon, objectives, and interview techniques employed in the child psychiatry clinic where they were to work.

Though this study does not appear to have any noteworthy

aspects from our current perspective, the important thing it emphasizes is that volunteers can function in child psychiatry agencies, and they can perform roles previously considered to be too technical—especially with the disturbed child and parents in a psychiatric clinic.

Youth in Social Work

Just as volunteer social work has been frequently reserved for people who have shown they have expertise in other fields, i.e. business, it also usually has been considered appropriate only for those who have attained maturity. One-to-one work with clients then has been conducted, for the most part, by those in their twenties or older, or possibly those just beginning college.

"A Community Program of Intergroup Activity for Youth," which was a project sponsored by a National Institute of Mental Health grant, showed that teenagers can be involved in volunteer programs as well (Perlmutter and Durham 1965). This early program utilizing youths as volunteers with youngsters, much the same as is done in "Big Brother" programs, was designated the PAL Program.

As in the case of the creation of other volunteer pilot programs, this one was an outgrowth of a recognition of the presence of a personnel shortage combined with a realization that new types of assistance should be instituted with the clients in question.

The population in this case was made up of elementary school children. These youngsters had come to the attention of the School Social Work Department in Champaign, Illinois. It was felt that these children could benefit from a healthy relationship with someone older than themselves.

With this situation present, the Champaign Youth Council (a citywide group composed of twenty-six teenage organizations) was approached for help. The opportunity this program presented to the youths who participated were two-fold: (1) they could find out what social work activities were like under one set of circumstances, and (2) they could become involved in a mature, interpersonal activity in which responsible actions on their part were a must.

However, as Felice Perlmutter and Dorothy Durham note in relation to this program, the structure and lines of control must be clear if the use of youthful workers is to be effective.

> The professional staff must be aware of the controls, both organizational and professional, that are called into play. Thus, the organizational controls must be developed to a maximum, while the more independent professional controls are used minimally. Accordingly, the structure developed for the Pal Program was designed to maximize the help available automatically in the situation:
>
> 1. Monthly group meetings were held for general supervisory purposes, but the teen-agers were encouraged to call the supervisor any time the need arose.
>
> 2. The size of the group was kept to eight members to assure full participation.
>
> 3. An age differential was established to minimize problems of identification and confusion between the teen-ager and the child. The teen-ager had to be 16 or over, while the child client was between 6 and 10 years of age.
>
> 4. A turnover of Pals was planned annually to protect the teen-ager from overinvolvement with the child's problems.
>
> 5. The program stopped during the summer, coinciding with the casework schedule.
>
> 6. Pals did not communicate directly with the casework staff, because this might be confusing to them. Rather, the supervisory staff served as a liaison between the Pals and the children's caseworkers. (P. 46)

In the above study, as well as in subsequent ones which serve to employ youths in innovative ways, the structure is an important element. Without it, the uncontrolled and somewhat immature teenager might put himself or herself and the younger client in a bad, possibly dangerous position. However, with the proper supervision and control, the creative employment of young, motivated volunteers in social work would seem to be a most promising undertaking.

PARAPROFESSIONALS IN SOCIAL WORK

Social work aides and technicians, as they are often referred to in the literature, have generally received positive evaluations.

Project ENABLE, for example, was a national project which sought to produce a program with maximum involvement—at every step of the way from planning to implementation—of the people from the very area and population for which it was intended to serve. A key feature of the program was to recruit and employ indigenous nonprofessionals as social work aides. The tentative findings of this study, as in the case of many of the early ones done in the mid-1960s, were generally positive (Birnbaum and Jones 1967).

While recognizing that since the program lasted only one year and the conclusions gained from observation should be evaluated "with brevity in mind." Martin Birnbaum and Chester H. Jones presented a number of impressions which support the use of indigenous nonprofessionals in social work. Among these thoughts was the belief that poor people are often unjustly categorized as "hard-core," "unmotivated," and "unreachable." Through the use of on-the-job training, they felt that people who were categorized in this way in the past could now channel their untapped talents into doing a variety of essential helping tasks.

Birnbaum and Jones also expressed their opinion that a sense of purpose, which is obtained either by the professional worker setting a role model or a purposeful goal given through training, is important for the workers to provide the direction and motivation for them to perform satisfactorily.

As a matter of fact, as in other studies in social work as well as in other disciplines, the positive influences of a well-structured nonprofessional program can have beneficial effects on the whole agency's staff. "Team functioning, in which professional and nonprofessional persons work cooperatively toward the achievement of common goals, provides a valuable structure for the development of positive interpersonal relationships and for growth and development for everyone involved" (Birnbaum and Jones 1967, p. 631).

Utilization of Indigenous Social Work Nonprofessionals

Specific and general reasons for employment of indigenous nonprofessionals in social work have been supported by a number of reports. One of these reports (Cudaback 1969), for instance, found that case sharing between line workers and nonprofessional ex-clients resulted in a good balance for the agency in terms of team resources.

The line workers who were the "hired professional helpers" learned a good deal from their nonprofessional counterparts. The line workers tended to be young, inexperienced college graduates who remained on the job for a relatively short amount of time. These new graduates reportedly gained a different perspective on the clients from their nonprofessional counterparts. In addition, the welfare service aides could actually facilitate the line workers' on-the-job training by helping them make the link between them-selves and the communities in which they served.

George Brager (1965) supports the above view that nonpro-fessionals can often bring to light a different perception of a client's problem which the middle-class worker might miss or fail to understand.

> Since they themselves have had extensive dealing with public services, indigenous workers tend to look askance at bureaucratic authority. In their service function as well they quickly see the barriers to the resolution of individual and community-wide problems stemming from organizational rigidity or disinterest. They are, fur-thermore, less interested in or sensitive to the maintenance require-ments of the agency that employs them. (Brager 1965, P. 38)

As well as reasons for employing indigenous nonprofessionals such as we have already covered, one emphasized by Frank Leowenberg (1968) was the therapeutic effect of employment on the workers themselves. As he aptly recognizes, "for those who have always been losers, gaining self respect, identity, and skill is no small achievement" (p. 66) .

Problems in Using Indigenous Nonprofessionals

As one might expect, there are also a number of problems and questions regarding the incorporation of nonprofessionals into the staff. In discussing some of the problems they believe are most prominent, Perry Levinson and Jeffry Schiller (1966) deal with the difficulties which arise around recruitment, training, use of authority, confidentiality, and personal identity.

Levinson and Schiller indicate that training fairly uneducated adults can be quite difficult, especially if the material deals with subtle aspects of interpersonal relations and the necessity of maintaining confidentiality—particularly when it involves the agency or their neighbors. Recruiting minority group members and teaching them to use their authority fairly can sometimes be a problem, also. Part of this may be due to their background and former role model as recipients of the system's "justice and supports." Finally, Levinson and Schiller point to the usual nemesis in any nonprofessional program, the problem that arises if and when the worker overidentifies with the agency and consequently loses touch with the community. Thus, while the employment of nonprofessionals in social work provides promise, as in other areas of human services, it is not without its problems as well.

Final Comments

Social work paraprofessionals and volunteers are part of the early new careers scene in the human services. Some of the most prominent initial papers on the use of nonprofessionals in the helping professions appeared in social work journals in the early 1960s.

Despite this early embrace of experimentation with the new careers concept, social work, like the other professions, still was marked by a sense of exclusivity that kept it from being open to paraprofessionals. For instance, the social work group almost was torn in two when the question came up as to whether bachelor's level practitioners should receive full membership with those possessing a master's degree in social work.

Social work is the ideal profession for experimentation in the use of new types of personnel in innovative roles. It is community-oriented by nature, and it has a history of being flexible and open to change, as well as being accepting of new ideas in helping people with their real, everyday problems. As a result, careful monitoring of past and current new careers programs is especially important in this area, for although social work is marked by some of the same archaic group membership exclusionary norms that other professions have, it is this association which has proven more amenable to change. Of all the professional groups, it is social work where nonprofessionals will probably get the greatest opportunity to do the most good.

REFERENCES

Birnbaum, M. L. and Jones, C. H.: Activities of social work aides. *Social Casework, 48*(10), 626-32, 1967.

Brager, George: The indigenous worker: a new approach to the social work technician. *Social Work, 10*(2), 33-40, 1965.

Cain, L. and Epstein, D.: The utilization of housewives as volunteer case aides. *Social Casework, 48*(5), 383-85, 1967.

Cudaback, Dorothea: Case sharing in the AFDC programs: the use of welfare service aides. *Social Work, 14*(3), 93-99, 1969.

Kraft, Irvin: Volunteers as social-work technicians in a child psychiatry clinic. *Mental Hygiene, 50*(3), 460-62, 1966.

Levinson, Perry and Schiller, Jeffry: Role analysis of the indigenous nonprofessional. *Social Work, 11*(3), 95-101, 1966.

Lowenberg, F. M.: Social workers and indigenous nonprofessionals: some structural dilemmas. *Social Work, 13*(3), 65-71, 1968.

Pearlmutter, F. and Durham, D.: Using teenagers to supplement casework service. *Social Work, 10*(2), 41-46, 1965.

Rosen, Alex: The pervasive shortage of professional personnel. *Children, 7,* 72, 1960.

Chapter 11

MEDICINE*

U SE OF ALLIED health personnel is not new. Physicians have long needed qualified and trained assistants to help them fill the medical requirements of American society. This need has not lessened, particularly in the city ghettos and in sparsely populated rural areas. One study (Young 1974), for instance, reports a steady decline in the number of physicians in Oklahoma communities of 25,000 people or less. This decline has not been dealt with by an actual or planned replacement of physician losses by new graduates. These findings are not isolated; unequal distribution of medical doctors is a reality in many parts of the nation.

To deal with this longstanding doctor shortage, most health centers employ an array of nonphysician professionals, such as registered nurses, and associate professionals, i.e. operating room technicians. In this respect the paraprofessional movement is not new. However, as Gartner (1971) recognizes, "What *is* new is that new activities are being performed, and more significant, old workers are being upgraded to new jobs" (p. 68).

NEW HEALTH PRACTITIONERS
Purpose

"New Health Practitioners" (NHPs) are expected—as members of a team—to be performing functions which will increase effective health care for greater numbers of people. How this is to be actually accomplished by new careerists and upgraded health workers currently in the system is naturally open to question; there is little agreement on the specific role NHPs are supposed to fill.

However, if two basic functions of NHPs could be agreed up-

---

*See also Appendix 9.

on by most people, they probably would be to (1) assist the physician in routine tasks and (2) perform currently usually non-existent health activities which medical doctors either do not have the time nor the resources to perform (Shindell and Cutler 1974).

> In performing one or the other of these functions, it is expected that the new health practitioner will perform preventive services and improve both communication with the patients served and compliance with recommended therapy, thereby increasing the effectiveness of the health care system. It is suggested that even if he doesn't do these things directly, he will free the physician from other tasks so that the physician will be able to accomplish these objectives. It is further suggested that for maximum effectiveness, the new health practitioner be integrated into a health care team. (Shindell and Cutler 1974, P. 123)

Acceptance by the Public and Physicians

The public are used to nonphysicians caring for them. Nurses, x-ray technicians, and lab workers are so much a part of the medical scene that little is made of their participation by the patient. One does not expect physicians in a modern hospital to perform every aspect of technical medical support and bedside care.

In upgrading these existing workers and adding new activities, via recently graduated medical careerists filling unique roles, the question does arise as to whether nonphysicians can be accepted if they perform roles traditionally reserved to medical doctors. In response to this question, a number of studies (Patterson 1969) have reported that new careerists such as physician's assistants (PAs) and pediatric nurse associates are accepted by much of the public.

Acceptance of NHPs by physicians is an issue as well. The questions a doctor might ponder in arriving at a decision as to whether or not to have an NHP (such as a PA) are—

1. Would I be personally comfortable delegating authority to an NHP?

2. What are the financial advantages and disadvantages involved in hiring an NHP?

3. How would this new worker fit into an existing/poten-
tially modifiable health organization?

4. What kind of knowledge can I expect this NHP to
possess?

5. Would use of a new health careerist be acceptable to
the population I serve?

6. What are the legal issues involved in having an NHP
working for me?

Of all the above questions, because of the rise in malpractice
insurance and the ever looming possibility of a criminal suit,
probably the thorniest question is the last one listed concerning
the legal implications involved in employing an NHP. This is
most relevant in regard to the PA, since this position is one with
a usually vague definition of skills and power.

Legal Issues and the Use of NHPs

"Certification," "licensure," and "regulation" are unappealing
terms to many in the forefront of the human services movement.
If anything, one of the primary impetuses of the movement was to
de-emphasize the stringent requirements of credentialed professional associations in favor of assembling a cadre of new careerists
less bound by organizational limits than by the talents and skills
they possess to help people medically, educationally, and psychologically (Wicks 1977).

In the health area, though, licensing of NHPs is still an
essential issue because of the financial risks involved. The employing physician is liable for injury/death which is the result of
negligent acts/omissions attributable to anyone he employs. With
soaring malpractice insurance it is no wonder that physicians are
concerned about the legal and financial implications of employing an NHP.

For instance, Frederick Hofmeister, in a testimony before the
Secretary's Commission on Malpractice on December 17, 1971,
said that while "it is essential that allied health personnel become
members of the health care delivery team. . . . The obstetrician/
Gynecologist is reluctant to use allied health personnel until
adequate protective mechanisms are formulated and until the

senate statutes recognize the expanded role of these personnel under the direction of the physician" (Department of Health, Education, and Welfare 1971).

Not all agree with Hofmeister. In the case of the physician's assistant, for example, one group (Sadler, Sadler, and Bliss 1972) feels that the use of PAs can actually *reduce* malpractice risks.

This group feels the proper use of PAs can accomplish this for two reasons: "First, effective utilizations of PAs will allow the physician to concentrate on those medical procedures and judgments that only he can manage. Second, a malpractice suit often results from poor patient rapport rather than negligence per se. When a patient is seen after a considerable wait and then only hurriedly by a harassed physician, the probability of patient dissatisfaction is magnified; . . . when a physician's assistant is used, waiting periods are reduced . . ." (p. 81).

Yet, while the above argument does take issue with the opinion that the risk of a malpractice suit is increased with the use of new health professionals, it does not speak to the issue of criminal liability. According to W. D. Stanhope (1974), "there is little disagreement among legal experts that in a state without specific legal sanctions, the NHP is at risk for charges of illegally practicing medicine and that the supervisory physician is also at risk for charges of aiding and abetting the illegal practice of medicine" (p. 118).

In the case of *People* versus *Whittaker* (1967), a legal precedent was seemingly set which greatly restricts the use of PAs until legislation is enacted to define the freedoms (and limitations) under which they can practice.

In the *Whittaker* case, a former Navy surgical technician and his employing neurosurgeon were found guilty of practicing medicine and aiding and abetting the illegal practice of medicine. Essentially, the charge was that the technician was not a physician and, therefore, had no right to act in any manner as one.

Recognizing the need for legislation requiring regulation, certification/licensure of physician's assistants is one thing, but accomplishing it is quite another. There are at least 130 separate health care occupation listings—most of them vaguely overlapping in their responsibilities and duties (Pennell and Hoover 1970). Consequently, even when criteria is set up for licensing of PAs —which is currently a pressing issue in many states—other existing professionals/paraprofessionals may meet the requirements as well. Such is the situation in some states in the case of PAs where the criteria is already met by nurses (Young 1974).

For the regulations governing the PAs and other New Health Practitioners to be clearly defined, with the patient's welfare as the main concern, care must be taken to study the factors involved so the laws do not become so restrictive as to defeat the NHP movement before it even has a chance to develop.

With this in mind it is important to ensure that the "right" people from diverse backgrounds are involved in setting up and administering the licensing of NHP's. In other words, these boards should not consist solely of members of current professions, i.e. American Medical Association, American Nursing Association, but should be an interdisciplinary group with representation from the very group they are delegated to oversee (Kane 1974). In this way, there can be a balance on the board between the existing professionals and assistants who have carried the burden of the health care operations on their shoulders until this point and the new careerists who are endeavoring to provide help for them, so greater numbers can receive increased attention and care.

PHYSICIAN'S ASSISTANT

Of all the new health careerists, one of the most controversial ones is the physician's assistant (PA). Part of the problem with this new role lies in the fact that the term remains ambiguous. As J. D. Wallace noted at the Twenty-fifth World Medical Assembly in 1971,

> The subject of this particular session, the Physician's assistant, should be of interest to all because that particular term appears to have caught the fancy of the whole health world during recent years. The only trouble is that every once in a while someone has the audacity to ask 'What is a Physician's Assistant anyway?' and then we're really in trouble. There appear to be as many definitions as there appear to be people making them.

Another difficulty that proponents of the PA movement are encountering is from within the nursing sector. One of the milder statements questioning the value of training PAs comes from Loretta Ford, a supporter of the nurse practitioner model (which is very similar to that of the PA). She says,

> Nursing has had a long history of numerous workers entering its field. The questionable quality of many of these people from a variety of training programs (they all profess to be doing the same job as professional nurses—caring for patients) deserves the attention of other professionals who are also preparing assistants . . . Medicine should profit from the experience of nursing and examine its efforts in preparing physician assistants who may, in the long run, offer more competition than cooperation and more challenge than collaboration. (Ford 1974, P. 6)

Despite such resistance to the utilization of PAs, the movement to train and employ them is still very much alive. Apparently, an appreciation of the problems of inefficient and insufficient health care in many of the nation's extremely populated and sparsely populated regions, as well as a recognition of the value of having new types of physician's extenders, has prompted ongoing support of the continued use of PAs.

The broad description by the American Medical Association (AMA) of the areas for PA employment can give one an idea of the potential utilization that these workers have as members of the health care team:

> The job description for the primary care PA, for example, identifies the following areas in which that PA may function: (a) diagnostic services; (b) continuing medical care for chronic disease and pregnancy; (c) care of acute disease and injury; (d) rehabilitation; (e) health maintenance; (f) health services to the community at large. (Department of Health Manpower, Division of Medical Practice, American Medical Association 1973, P. 6)

Many factors about the PA's role definition, training, employment, supervision, acceptance (by patients, physicians, and nurses), salary, and insurance coverage continue to be debated. Although the American Medical Association is addressing itself to these questions, the solutions thus far attained are still tenuous and vague. As a result, attention will have to be given to the

AMA proposals in future years, which will help clarify the position of the physician's assistant. Likewise, any steps taken by individual hospitals (see Fig. 11-1), organizations, individual states, or other associations/governing bodies in an effort to help solidify the P.A. concept will merit watching.

If the P.A. role develops into one like the "Soviet Feldhers" who serve in the U.S.S.R. as second rate doctors good enough to serve the poor and disadvantaged, but not good enough to help the affluent, the PA's destiny will be questionable (Storey 1972). However, if the new careerist can develop a role and achieve in it, the impact on the health care of the general public and the health care delivery system can be most impressive.

Job Description of PA on Muskogee V.A. Hospital Medical Service

---

Principal Duties and Responsibilities:

Professional—The incumbent must be a graduate of an approved program for Physician's Assistants and duly registered by the American Academy of Physicians' Assistants and perform all of the following duties:

1. Performs initial history and physical evaluations and 2507's on new in-patients and out-patients, establishes presumptive diagnoses, establishes general work-up of patients by ordering appropriate laboratory studies, performs routine incisions and drainages, wound care and debridement, nasogastric intubations, gastric analysis lumbar punctures, sutures lacerations, etc., the majority of which are performed directly or indirectly under physician supervision.
2. Performs diagnostic tests such as insulin and I.V. glucose tolerance tests and tolbutamide tests, tissue biopsies, lumbar punctures, paracentesis, thoracentesis, and other procedures in consultation with the physician.
3. Places indwelling arterial catheters and performs the necessary blood gas analysis.
4. Starts whole blood.
5. Starts I.V. solutions.
6. Administers emergency medications.
7. Manages cardiac arrest patients until attending physician is present.

8. Manages acute respiratory failure until attending physician is present.

9. Manages life endangering traumatic injuries until the attending physician is present.

10. Administers intravenous medications when necessary.

11. Assists the physician in planning, organizing, and delivering orderly medical management programs for patients under his care.

12. Arranges consultations and sees that patients are correctly scheduled for special tests.

13. Is available on call to any area in the hospital during his tour of duty to assist in any emergent patient care situation that may arise.

14. Is thoroughly familiar with all current diagnostic, therapeutic, clinical, and medical management techniques.

Figure 11-1. Example of a listing of physician's assistants' duties and responsibilities.

COMMUNITY/HOME HEALTH AIDE

The PA position is a classical example of where the NHP movement is going with regards to those new careerists possessing at least a high school diploma and—in most cases—possibly some advanced technical or college level training. Naturally, though, the NHP movement is not confined to the utilization of only personnel at this higher educational level.

New careers in health are also being explored for the socioeconomically disadvantaged, the inexperienced, and the educationally deprived, i.e. persons not possessing high school level skills. An example of a position within this scope which aptly illustrates the direction of the movement is the community/home health aide.

The rationale for the need to develop the position of community/home health aide and ones like it are based on the following assumptions:

1. The growing need for expanded health services throughout the country requires a corresponding increase in the number of people who have been trained and who are qualified to meet this service need.

2. Given the necessary job and career opportunity, support, and training, the unemployed, underemployed, and disadvantaged of our nation can effectively fill these positions and participate in programs that are designed to raise the delivery capability of health services to optimum level.

3. People who are recruited from the area being served provide an effective and unique link between the community and the health agency, thereby enhancing the effectiveness of the agency in which the workers are employed.

4. Using New Careers subprofessionals in an integrated program of health services frees the professional to work more effectively.

5. Real Job opportunities and training provide an important answer to the need of the disadvantaged for motivation, involvement, training, and careers with growth potential. (New Careers Institute 1968)

The community health aide (CHA) performs a number of specific and varied functions (see Fig. 11-2). In general, this position differs from the home aide; the CHA "is concerned with family health needs, with environmental health, and with those community organizations that function to protect and improve the health of the public. The home health aide's primary concern is meeting individual health needs in the home setting— giving bedside care and establishing and maintaining a milieu of therapeutic and preventive care for a physically and/or mentally ill patient in her care" (New Careers Institute 1958, p. 1).

The key factor in the CHA position which makes it stand out is the role it plays in increasing the community's use of local health resources. As Reiff and Reissman (1964) and others (Cornely and Bigman 1961; Kent and Smith 1967; Sobey 1970) recognized, this function was extremely essential in ensuring the proper utilization of local health care facilities.

Unless there is a cadre of workers who speak the language of the community, all the professional publicity in the world will not achieve optimal results. To bridge suspicion and correct health misinformation, the most useful workers are people the community can relate to and understand. Such is the role of the community/home health aides.

Community Health Aide Functions:

Cornely and Bigman state that a person at the "practical" level is needed to reach low-income families. Such a person would come from the same environment as the families served, talk their language, be well acquainted with the "gatekeepers," and able to develop meaningful contacts through nonverbal communications. This community health aide would receive professional direction from well-qualified health workers who provide him with accurate information that he can present in laymen's patterns of language and in terms of their health knowledge and attitudes Reiff and Riessman described this "expediter" role as a ink between the client and the community' professional health resources.

Here are the functions of the *community health aide:*

1. Motivates patients and families to seek health care — providing support, showing interest, conveying understanding, maintaining a friendly relationship, and using other neighborly techniques.
2. Interprets the importance of seeking preventive care and early treatment of disease.
3. Instructs individuals in the home and in groups regarding primary prevention (all those measures that promote health such as proper nutrition, good personal hygiene, good housekeeping practices, proper rest, adequate ventilation, adequate exercise, etc.).
4. Assists in evaluating the health needs of each family member under close supervision of his supervisor, for example, by referral to appropriate agencies of a mother who needs prenatal care; a school-age child who needs eye or dental care; a father who needs a physical examination; a grandmother who needs follow-up care for her known diabetic condition; a preschool child who never had child health supervision, or a child who appears mentally retarded and should be examined.
5. Assists in determining priorities of health needs and in developing a plan of care, under the close supervision of the health aide trainer/supervisor.
6. Informs the family of available community health facilities where their specific needs can be met.
7. Assists in interpreting the eligibility requirements of various health facilities to families.

8. Assists in making referrals to the appropriate health agency regarding care plans; ascertains whether the patient has actually obtained the service to which he was referred.

9. Accompanies a patient to the health facility when necessary.

10. Attends patients' children or elderly relatives in their home while the patient obtains care at a health facility.

11. Reports to the public health nurse, social workers, physician and oher professionals significant findings in relation to health and social matters that come to his attention during the performance of his duties.

12. When appropriate, reinforces the instructions given by the professional and encourages the patient to follow orders.

13. Seeks persons in the neighborhood who have unattended health problems and initiates appropriate action.

14. Maintains an accurate record of contracts with families and of the services that have been provided.

15. Initiates, organizes and assists in implementing a program of health education classes under the supervision of the health aide trainer/supervisor.

16. Aids in initiating, organizing and implementing activities to motivate large numbers of persons to avail themselves of health services and health innovations, (e.g., mass immunization programs, x-ray screening programs, etc.).

17. Teaches the family sound housekeeping practices, accident prevention, good nutritional habits, and personal hygiene in order to bring about a more healthful life.

18. May perform some housekeeping duties while attending children or elderly relatives while other members of the family obtain care at a health facility. This most often involves preparing food and dressing infants and preschoolers.

19. Performs first aid measures when appropriate.

20. Helps specialist develop health literature directed to the educational level of the target population.

21. Participates in team conferences with professional staff regarding individual families.

Figure 11-2. A listing of functions of a community health aide. Source: New Careers Institute, University Research Corporation: *The Community/ Home Health Aide Trainer's Manual.* New Careers Institute, Washington, D.C., 1968. (Preparation and distribution of manual was provided for through contract with the U.S. Department of Labor, Manpower Administration, Bureau of Work-Training Programs.)

OTHER ALLIED HEALTH PROFESSIONS

As well as the community/home health aide, nurse practitioner, and physician assistant positions, there is an array of other health professions that have had an impact on the current health scene. Three of the more prominent of these are the medical technologist, the respiratory therapist, and the radiologic technologist.

The *medical technologist* utilizes advanced laboratory equipment. This position involves the worker in medical diagnosis and in the evaluation of the current therapy being employed with a given patient. As a medical technologist, the person may work in a medical center, physician's office, hospital, community clinic, research center, or public health agency. To qualify for this position, many schools have developed four-year college programs with a curriculum emphasizing chemistry and the biological sciences.

As a *respiratory therapist,* a person can work in various medical settings. Prior to qualification for registration, the respiratory therapist must receive didactic, laboratory, and clinical training in pulmonary functioning. This is presently one of the largest growing areas in the allied health field.

Radiologic technicians are trained to qualify for certification by the American Registry of Radiologic Technologists. This position has been around for a number of years, but only lately has it developed into a really meaningful and accepted, sophisticated career. The training under radiologists (M.D.s) and experienced technicians is related to the handling of patients when taking their x-rays. In addition, today special attention is being given to learning about those instruments used during surgical radiologic diagnostic studies—an area that is continually advancing in sophistication and complexity.

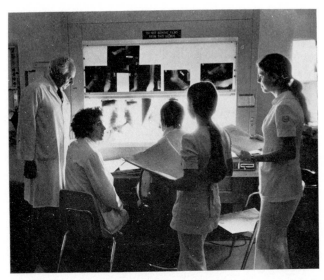

Figure 11-3. Radiology technicians receiving personal instruction in reading x-rays. (Photo courtesy of Hahnemann Medical College & Hospital Philadelphia.)

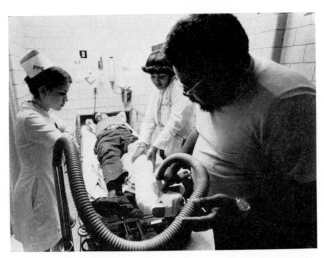

Figure 11-4. Physicians' assistants at work in a hospital emergency room. (Photo courtesy of Hahnemann Medical College & Hospital, Philadelphia.)

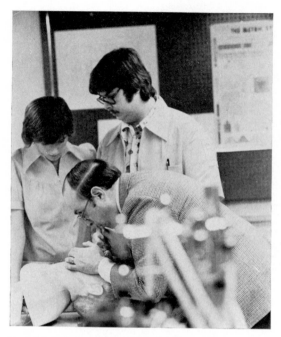

Figure 11-5. Respiration therapists receive instruction from a physician using a model to demonstrate resuscitation technique. (Photo courtesy of Hahnemann Medical College & Hospital, Philadelphia.)

Final Comments

The dawning of the new health practitioner (NHP) movement has brought with it as many questions as it has answers. In the beginning, the major impetus for its development was—as in other human services areas—the crying need for more qualified personnel to help raise the nation's health standards. Since then the NHP movement has been bogged down in a mire of red tape and resistance on the part of some professional groups. As in the case of the swine flu vaccine in 1976, we seem to believe we have the preventive medicine we need, but the bureaucracy and certain interest groups are holding the program back.

Some of the apparent reasons for the halting of the NHP program are as follows:

Figure 11-6. Physician's assistants discussing the medical procedures that were used in the emergency room. (Photo courtesy of Hahnemann Medical College & Hospital.)

1. Some NHP titles have vague role definitions, thus leading to confusion regarding training, certification/licensing, and fears by some groups, i.e. nurses, regarding the potential encroachment by new professionals, such as physician's assistants.

2. There is no legal definition as to how far an NHP can go in exercising clinical judgment and ordering subsequent treatments.

3. The threat of malpractice suits inhibits professionals who might use NHPs.

4. There is a lack of reimbursement (third party payments) for treatments provided by some NHPs.

5. Opportunities for new careerists are not being established by hospitals and clinics to accommodate the new health professional, nor are they being altered to be set up in accordance with the new team concept in medical care.

Some groups have begun to deal with these problems at least by formulating guidelines and recommendations on how to deal with the new health worker (see Fig. 11-3). Still, much remains to be done. The unfortunate aspect is that unless far reaching steps are taken soon, the new health practitioner movement's life may be cut short by the very professional groups who originally clamored for their creation.

Recommendations From A Conference On New Health Practitioners*

The following recommendations were approved by a majority of the conference participants:

1. The plurality of types of new health practitioners should be recognized and all steps taken to eliminate jurisdictional disputes and interdisciplinary rivalries.
2. Departments of Community and/or Preventive Medicine should undertake studies to identify both consumer needs and demands in regard to new health practitioners and their roles in the delivery of health care.
3. Departments of Community and/or Preventive Medicine should undertake studies to define the performance patterns of nurse practitioners and physician assistants to determine the extent to which these new health practitioners perform the same and different functions in various settings.
4. Departments of Community and/or Preventive Medicine should study various configurations for the delivery of health care services in rural and urban areas to identify alternative models of delivery.
5. Medical schools should be encouraged to develop and operate health care delivery systems which incorporate the use of new health practitioners.
6. Medical school curricula should include information on the

quality of care and the effects of new health practitioners on that quality.

7. Education of medical students and other health professional students should include exposure to the role of new health professionals. NHP's might be trained alongside the health professionals or serve as teachers for these other health professionals.

8. Medical schools should reexamine their admissions procedures to consider the problems of recruiting individualists as future physicians who will be working in health care teams.

9. New health practitioner programs should continue to follow their graduates not only in terms of evaluating clinical competence and providing continuing education, but also to learn more about the problems involved in introducing the new health practitioner into a practice setting. The new health practitioner should be recognized as an organizational strategy to effect changes in organization patterns and physician behavior.

10. Departments of Community and/or Preventive Medicine should pay more attention to organization theory and its applications with particular reference to the introduction of new health care personnel.

11. Planning for the continued use of new health practitioners should carefully consider the options available in terms of the real world constraints of today.

12. The expansion of new health practitioner training programs should be tempered by substantial investment in research to identify ways in which new health practitioners have been employed and the effects such employment has had on the health care delivery systems.

13. New health practitioner programs should emphasize quality of training in order to assure adequate mobility of graduates.

14. Additional proliferation of training programs of any sort should be very carefully considered for quality and projected demands for graduates.

15. At this point in time pluralism should be encouraged in the approach to the preparation of new health practitioners; a variety of approaches should be supported, identifying the relative values for various situational factors.

16. Policy in regard to the training of new health professionals

should include a continuum which includes the evaluation of existing plural diversified models, the identification of concepts and methodologies which could be consolidated in the development of operational programs based on these which could develop NHP's in the numbers needed. Additional feedback is then necessary to provide "mid-course corrections" to the operational training models.

17. There is a need for careful evaluation of the use of new health practitioners in terms of various models for reimbursement, health care settings, etc.

18. Evaluation should include controlled studies to reinforce the external validity of internally-valid concepts that have already been established in clinical trials with new health practitioners thus far. These studies would take the form of surveillance on a long-term basis utilizing a small number of selected variables.

19. Evaluation data should be gathered in a comparable fashion across programs to examine the large variety of new health professionals. Such an assessment will help to answer certain questions of importance in planning, in altering educational programs, and in making decisions about future regulations.

20. As evaluators of NHP's, Departments of Community and/or Preventive Medicine should avoid becoming overly attached to any single new concept or approach and maintain an open mind.

21. There is a need for trend data in terms of supply and demand for new health manpower.

Figure 11-7. (No legend; in source).

REFERENCES

American Medical Association, Department of Health Manpower, Division of Medical Practice: *Employment and Use of Physicians Assistants; A Guide for Physicians,* 1973.

Cornely, Paul and Bigman, Stanley: *Cultural Considerations in Changing Health Attitudes.* Howard Univ. College of Medicine, Washington, D.C.

Ford, Loretta C.: Health care: who will lead the way? In Kane, Robert

---

*Conference sponsored by The John E. Fogarty International Center for the Advanced Study in the Health Sciences and the Association of the Teachers of Preventive Medicine, National Institute of Mental Health, Bethesda, Maryland, May 14–15, 1974.

L. (Ed.): *New Health Practitioners.* National Institute of Health, Bethesda, Maryland, 1974.

Gartner, Alan: Health. In Gartner (Ed.): *Paraprofessionals and Their Performance.* Praeger, New York, 1971.

Kane, Robert L. (Ed.): *New Health Practitioners.* The John E. Fogarty International Center for the Advanced Study in the Health Services and the Association of Teachers of Preventive Medicine, National Institute of Health, Bethesda, Maryland, 1974.

New Careers Institute (NCI): *New Careers: The Community/Home Health Aide Trainer's Manual.* NCI, Washington, D.C., 1968.

People v. Whittaker, (Sup. Ct. 1967) Shasta County, California.

Reiff, Robert and Reissman, Frank: *The Indigenous Nonprofessional.* National Institute of Labor Education, New York, 1964.

Sadler, A. M., Sadler, B. L., and Blum, A. A.: *The Physician's Assistants: Today and Tomorrow.* Yale Univ. Press, New Haven, Conn., 1972.

Shindell, Sidney and Cutler, Jeffrey, A.: Regulation, certification, and licensure of the new health practitioner. In *New Health Practitioners.*

Sobey, Francine: *The Nonprofessional Revolution in Mental Health* Columbia Univ. Press, New York, 1970.

Stanhope, William D.: What's a person going to do with an extra pair of right hands? or the utilization of the new health practitioner. In *New Health Practitioners.*

Storey, Patrick B.: *The Soviet Feldher as a Physician's Assistant: A Guide for Physicians,* 1973.

U.S. Department of Health, Education, and Welfare: *Expanding the Scope of Nursing Practitioners—A Report of the Secretary's Committee To Study Extended Poles for Nurses.* Washington, D.C., 1973.

Wicks, Robert J.: *Counseling Strategies and Intervention Techniques for the Human Services.* Lippincott, Philadelphia, 1977.

Young, E. W.: Personal communication. In *New Health Practitioners.*

Chapter 12

IMPLICATIONS FOR THE FUTURE
IN THE HUMAN SERVICES:
SOME FINAL COMMENTS

FROM THIS book one can get some indication of the complexion of the new careers movement as it exists today in the various systems within the human services field. But what of tomorrow? Where must we move to continue progressing? At what point are we at this time?

By viewing the past twenty years, one might well agree that the 1960s and early 1970s were revolutionary times in the human services. In sharp contrast to the previous periods in mental health, these years marked the dawning and development of the nonprofessional revolution in mental health.

On the positive side, this most recent period in the human services history saw the following:

1. Greater application of public health principals to the mental health field.

2. Recognition of the social and economic forces that were taking place to cut off many categories of people from the work force.

3. Special efforts to recruit, screen, train, and place non-professionals—particularly indigenous ones—in criminal justice, social work, education, medicine, and mental health.

4. Development of career ladders for nonprofessionals.

5. Acceptance of the value community members have in teaching professionals how to better deal with the reality-oriented, environmental problems of people from certain geographic locales and socioeconomic groups.

6. Creation of new innovative programs in community mental health.

Tempering these generally good outcomes, however, were

several shortcomings. One of the negative outcomes was that, with the creative expansion of new careers, came also a good deal of confusion concerning the individual role definition of these new workers. This was a real problem in the health field where many legal and financial issues were at stake.

Another problematic aspect of the new careers movement was the future status of paraprofessional programs. Would funding continue after federal support was taken away? Could a nonprofessional eventually move into a professional slot in a project? If so, how would this be done? Would the nonprofessionals become useless as links with the community once they moved up the career ladder after programs had become established? And if the nonprofessionals do stay welded to the people they are to serve, can this be accomplished without eventually developing anti-professional attitudes?

Also, what of the credentials of new professionals? Unless some system is developed, paraprofessionals will be excluded from acceptance as *reimbursable providers*. If there is an appreciation for the need for some type of credentials, how is it to be accomplished? Will it be by attendance in a college/institutionally accredited course, through a competency examination, or by establishing some association which can set up standards which the new worker must meet?

Accrediting paraprofessionals is a crucial, complex issue that can lead to problems. For instance, once we get involved in setting up standards, much of the flexibility involved in paraprofessional training and employment is hampered. Furthermore, by putting the nonprofessional into a position of getting involved in a fee-for-services role, this worker is then put into competition with professionals already receiving payments. It is obvious, then, that the giving of credentials to nonprofessionals is going to have to be one of the primary questions that leaders in the human services field will have to grapple with in the near future.

The community mental health movement has also produced many questions. While providing facilities out in the community so the population of state hospitals could be lessened, the services provided out in the street have often proved insufficient. Aftercare was supposed to consist of a sophisticated system of therapies and rehabilitative modalities. In reality, often it now consists only of drug maintenance and a life alone for the patient in a second-rate boarding house.

Final Comments

Not only the paraprofessional movement but the overall community mental health movement is in question today. The still remaining fears of some professionals that they will be disregarded and replaced by a new cadre of nonprofessionals adds fuel to the concern about the effectiveness of modern mental health technologies; some would have us return to an exclusive use of the medical model.

But this is not the time to turn back. It is also not the time to separate forces so that the nonprofessionals are left on their own to minister to the poor and the professionals given the task of dealing exclusively with the more economically advantaged.

Since we are now in a position to better evaluate the efforts of community mental health and its nonprofessional workers, it *is* time now to be more creative. Also, since the new careerist is becoming more established as a part of the helping scene, it *is* now time to integrate professionals and nonprofessionals into a more systematic, well-organized team; some programs have begun such efforts, but we must be willing to experiment further.

Experimentation and modification are the keys. The problems of our people are not going to remain static. Likewise, entrenchment may make a few health professionals feel secure during this current time of rapid change, but to stop now would end in failure. Considering that what is at stake here is the human welfare of our people, this "solution," and other equally undaring ones, are totally unacceptable.

APPENDICES

Appendix 1

SUMMARY OF LEGISLATION AFFECTING UTILIZATION OF PARAPROFESSIONAL WORKERS*

Year	Legislation	Summary
1962	Manpower Development and Training Act (MDTA)	Authorized programs for training and re-training unemployed youth. Applied also to workers facing job displacement due to technological and economic changes. Programs were to be carried out by vocational, technical, and junior college level institutions.
1963	Vocational Education Act	Specifically addressed to the preparation for employment. Called for occupational training to be realistically related to changes in employment opportunities. Objective was to relate vocational education more closely to emerging occupations and industries and less to agricultural acitvities. Set up cooperative relationships between the employment service (USES) and vocational education systems. Provided for the exchange of information on hiring practices to be used in curriculum design.
1963	Amendments to MDTA	Concentrated on overcoming restrictions and exclusions in Act of 1962. Increased the training allowances for young trainees, lowered the original MDTA eligibility age (from 17 to 16), extended training duration (from 52 to 72 weeks). Placed heavier emphasis on basic literacy skills.
1964	Economic Opportunity Act (EOA)	Legislation authorizing War on Poverty. Provided expanded services and job opportunities to poverty populations. Emphasized and required evidence of participation of the poor in programs funded under Act. Fostered administrative machinery which bypassed

*Source: Department of Health, Education, and Welfare, Social Rehabilitation, Service Research Report No. 3. *Overview Study of Employment of Paraprofessionals,* U.S. Government Printing Office, Washington, D.C., 1974.

Year	Legislation	Summary
		established state and federal channels by designating Community Action organizations and planning councils as recipients of funds.
1965	Amendments to EOA (Nelson Amendments)	Provided employment for elderly poor people in conservation and community beautification activities.
1965	Amendments to EOA (Scheuer Amendments)	Specifically directed to the chronically unemployed adult over 21 years of age. Provided entry level employment in the public service sector in other than professional positions. Required that program plans contain provisions for training and advancement.
1966	Allied Health Professions Training Act	Made provisions for grants for training new types of health technologists and technicians.
1967	Amendments to EOA	Expanded population eligible for programs set up under the 1966 Scheuer Amendments. Reduced the eligible age for adults to 18 years of age or older. Made both unemployed and low income people eligible for jobs in programs. Placed additional emphasis on New Career opportunities in fields such as health, education, welfare, neighborhood redevelopment, and public safety.
1967	Amendments to Higher Education Act	Provided for programs or projects to train teacher aides or other paraprofessional educational personnel.
1967	Amendments to the Elementary and Secondary Education Act	Encouraged maximum hiring and adequate utilization and acceptance of auxiliary personnel (e.g., teacher aides) on a permanent basis in both elementary and secondary schools.
1967	Amendments to the Social Security Act (Harris Amendments)	Required that state plans submitted by public welfare agencies be modified to include provisions for the training and effective use of paid subprofessional staff, with particular emphasis on the full-time and part-time employment of recipients and other persons of low income.
1968	Amendments to the Vocational Education Act	Encouraged research and training in vocational education programs designed to meet special vocational education needs of young people. Provided educational opportunities for new and emerging careers in fields such as mental and physical health, crime pre-

Year	Legislation	Summary
		vention and corrections, welfare, education, municipal services, child care, and recreation. Placed particular emphasis on entry positions requiring less than professional education.
1968	Omnibus Crime Control and Safe Streets Act	Authorized grant programs to provide training as community service officers for residents of specific localities who did not meet police department entrance standards. Programs were directed toward police-community relations.
1968	Amendments to the Juvenile Delinquency and Control Act	Provided for the development of special programs to train young people and adults in diagnosis, treatment and rehabilitation of youths who were in danger of becoming delinquent.
1968	Health Manpower Act	Authorized special project grants to assist schools of medicine, dentistry, osteopathy, pharmacy, optometry, podiatry, and veterinary medicine to develop training for new levels or new types of personnel.
1968	Amendments to the Vocational Rehabilitation Act	Provided for special project grants to state VRA and other non-profit (public or private) agencies to stimulate use of paraprofessional New Careerists in rehabilitative services and to create New Career opportunities for the handicapped being served by VR agencies.
1969	Amendments to EOA	Created a special title (Title I-E) for New Careers programs and separated them from other manpower programs.

Appendix 2

PARAPROFESSIONAL SELECTION VARIABLES AND METHODS*

Source	Types of Workers	Selection Variables	Method(s) of Assessment
Anthony and Wain (1970)	Aide therapists	Empathy; non-possessive warmth; genuineness.	Ratings of behavior.
Berryman (1968)	Recreation aides	Interest in working with disadvantaged and handicapped; high school diploma, equivalence, or willingness to work for degree.	Counselor interviews.
Birnbaum and Jones (1967)	Social work aides	Aggressiveness; alertness; verbal ability; ability to read and write.	Applicant's ability to complete application forms.
Brager (1965)	Social technicians	Expertise in agency's programs; closely identify with own culture group; action-oriented.	†
Brecher, Kilguss, and Stewart (1968)	Day care aides	Interest; sound health (mental and physical); ability to care for children (should have child 14 years or older).	Interviews.

*Source: Department of Health, Education, and Welfare, Social Rehabilitation Service Research Report No. 3. *Overview Study of Employment of Paraprofessionals,* U.S. Government Printing Office, Washington, D. C., 1974.

†Data not provided.

Bucher, et al. (1968)	†	Interest; good mental and physical health; ability to find child care facilities.	Psychological interviews; indices measuring planning for future.
Cain and Epstein (1967)	Case aides	Interest; intelligence; empathy.	†
Calnan (1967)	Neighborhood aides	Income below the poverty level; location of home within walking distance of people served; participation in neighborhood affairs, e.g., PTA membership.	Completion of a written application form; kept appointment for job interview; presentation of self in job interview.
Coate and Nordstrom (1969)	Home health aides	High school education; 25 years or older; evidence of reliability and honesty; fairly stable home situation; experience in working with people; ability to relate positively; hospital experience.	†
Coggs and Robinson (1967)	Lay workers (in social work)	Experience in volunteer work; above-average knowledge of people; high self-worth; experience in working as an individual; involvement in neighborhood and civic groups.	†
Elston (1967)	Case aides	Ability to communicate; bilingual fluency; able to read and write; eighth grade education.	†
Grant (1967)	Community resource aides	21 years or older; passing a standard physical examination; ability to read, write, and speak English; ability to communicate with people from different walks of life; possession of a driver's license.	†

Source	Types of Workers	Selection Variables	Method(s) of Assessment
	Health aides	21 years or older; eighth grade education; residence in neighborhood for 1 year; able to follow written and oral directions; possession of a driver's license; able to maintain simple records.	†
	Social welfare aides	All of the above as well as: origin from low-income family; one year's experience working with problem people.	†
	Rehabilitation aides	Experience within past 10 years, either paid or unpaid, which has provided understanding and acceptance of disabled or disadvantaged people.	†
Grosser (1969b)	†	A quickness of mind and a capacity for growth with a public capability to lead and organize.	†
	†	Ability to prepare written reports; ability to participate in staff meetings and conferences; should not overidentify with client.	†
	†	A strong personality and a strong commitment to the agency.	†
	Homemaking aides	Homemaking skills; mastery of intricacies of urban slum living; good feeling toward people.	†

	Community workers	Local residence; prior work experience; participation in community organizations (e.g., PTA, union) ; maturity; ability to work with people; agency loyalty; participation in personal upgrading; willingness to undertake training; high school education or potential for GED.	†
	Direct service workers	Ability to communicate with clients through common language or style; empathy with client through shared life experience; ability to help clients negotiate complexities of the ghetto.	†
	Indigenous nonprofessionals (general)	Mutual interests with community residents; poor; residence in neighborhood served; minority group status; common background and language.	†
Hiland (1968)	Public welfare aides	At least a fifth grade education; work experience not needed; does not have to have clean police record; no serious health problems; empathy for clients.	Ratings by staff.
Committee on Effective Utilization of the Rehabilitation Counselor and Supporting Staff (1968)	Rehabilitation aides, including technical aides and indigenous aides	Age; educational level; ethnic background; community service; previous work history; vocational skills; salary expectation; status as a client. Demonstrated ability in interpersonal relationships; relatively good knowledge of the community; acceptance by the community; sufficient formal training to demonstrate an ability to learn; adequate free time from responsibilities; means for getting about community or work area.	Application forms.

Source	Types of Workers	Selection Variables	Method(s) of Assessment
National Social Welfare Assembly (1959)	Case aides	High school degree; aptitude for dealing with social relationships; emotional stability.	†
Neff (1965)	Workshop personnel	Practical experience in workshop of social work; good mental and physical health; get along with and be accepted by people.	Aptitude and dexterity tests.
Office of Career Development (1971)	Community developers	Strong preference for community development; previous involvement in community action; interest in pursuing academic degree with urban affairs interest.	†
Office of State Merit Systems, HEW (1968)	Human services workers	Understanding of disadvantaged persons; ability to communicate with persons to be served, to win their confidence, to help them, to influence them; adaptability; dependability; perseverance.	Questionnaires: questions about knowledge of poverty; case-worker report form on welfare recipient's occupational potentials; structured reference report for human services support classes.
		Ability to learn technical aspects of the job and potential for advancement with training.	Interviews: structured panel interview for human services support classes; structured group discussion for human services support classes.
			Tests: following directions; task; oral instructions; and adult literacy tests.
Reiff and Riessman (1964)	Community workers	Roots and interests in community; positive attitude toward community; ability to work with others; acceptance of supervision; desire and capacity to learn.	†

Riessman (1965a)	†	Does not have too strong client identification or over active need to please client.	†
Riley and Fellin (1970)	†	Motivation for upward mobility; potential for growth; adaptable to agency; concern for community problems; ability to communicate; ability to work with agency staff.	(Specifically excluded written tests).
Schmais (1967)	†	Involvement in community affairs; interest in the problems the agency deals with; contact with the community or neighborhood; ability to relate to people; social maturity; potential leadership qualities.	Application blanks; group interviews; selection panels.
Truax (1965)	Aide therapists	Empathy; non-possessive warmth; genuineness.	Ratings of behavior.
University Research Corporation (1970)	Home health aides	Indigenous to community; appreciation of hardships of clients; accepted by community; interest in others in community; ability to read and write; ability to give instructions to others.	†

BASIC DEMOGRAPHIC DATA OF PARAPROFESSIONALS (Selected Studies)*

Source	Setting or Program	Number of Persons	Demographic Variables				
			Age	Sex	Race	Educational Level	Income (SES)
Adelson & Kovner (1969)	Social health technician training program (Lower Manhattan)	41	†	Majority female	Majority black	Most less than high school	All low income
Ahearn (1969)	Two large New England Community Action Programs	112	21-50	50 percent female	Mostly black	†	†
Berryman (1968)	Neighborhood Youth Corps programs	75	Avg. 22	78 percent female	†	60 percent high school graduates	†
Birnbaum & Jones (1967)	Social work aides (former clients) in 59 Project Enable programs	†	†	†	†	Most less than high school	Many on welfare

*Source: Department of Health, Education, and Welfare, Social Rehabilitation Service Research Report No. 3. Overview Study of Employment of Paraprofessionals, U.S. Government Printing Office, Washington, D.C., 1974.
†Data not given.

Study	Program/Setting	N	Age	Sex	Race	Education	SES/Class
Brecher, et al. (1968)	Anti-poverty program participants in New England	38	22-61	Majority female	Mostly Irish-Italian	Average 10 years	Poor AFDC recipients
Cain & Epstein (1967)	Large metropolitan state hospital in New England (case aides)	25	25-55	100 percent female	†	45 percent had college	Middle class
Denham & Shatz (1969)	Human services agencies (Washington, D.C.)	150	†	†	Black	†	Underprivileged
Gannon (1968)	Harlem Domestic Peace Corps	150	Avg. 22.7	71 percent female	Black	High school graduates	†
Grosser (1965)	Mobilization for Youth program (Manhattan)	40	†	†	35 percent black, 40 percent Puerto Rican	82 percent high school or less	Many raised in slum areas (multidimensional SES index)
Harvey, et al. (1968)	Rehabilitation aides (Contra Costa, Calif.)	69	21-50	†	Most Mexican-Americans	Many 2-4 years college	†
Larson, et al. (1969)	New Careers Trainees (dropouts)	102	Avg. 31.5	52 percent male	59 percent non-white	Average 11-12 years	†
Lowenberg (1968)	Community Action and social service programs	38	†	†	95 percent non-white	Less than high school	†
Committee on Effective Utilization of Rehabilitation Counselor and Supporting Staff (1968)	Survey of 91 state VR agencies	297	18-65	55 percent female	†	Most high school	†

Source	Setting or Program	Number of Persons	Demographic Variables				
			Age	Sex	Race	Educational Level	Income (SES)
National Social Welfare Assembly (1966)	Client staff	†	21-72	†	Bilingual	†	Have experienced poverty
Perlmutter & Durham (1965)	Casework service aides	†	16+	†	†	High school	Suburban background
Shostak (1966)	Community program participants (Philadelphia)	†	†	†	55 percent white, 5 percent Puerto Rican	†	Less than $3,000/year
ORDT (1970)	National survey of SRS program agencies	10,547	Avg. late 30's	84 percent female	†	Majority high school graduates or G.E.D.	Many former public assistance recipients
Staub & Petree (1967)	Rehabilitation aides in out-patient clinic	5	†	†	†	High school	Middle class
Truax & Shapiro (1966)	Counselor aides	5	28-50	80 percent female	†	2 years of high school	†
Wilson, et al., (1969)	New Careers programs in 49 cities	7,000	22-34	80 percent female	74 percent black	48 percent high school or less	82 percent with less than $3,000 a year
Zurcher (1968)	OEO indigenous leaders	18	†	61 percent female	Most black, Mexican, Indian	†	Poor

Appendix 4

DESCRIPTION OF A MENTAL HEALTH TECHNOLOGY PROGRAM*

Career Description

THE MENTAL HEALTH TECHNOLOGIST is prepared to perform a diversity of tasks within the matrix of service delivery in the mental health field. The technologist will carry responsibilities to a degree commensurate with his middle-level professional education, involving direct patient care and contact with the families of patients. The core of his contribution will flow from his therapeutic skills, but will include functions ranging along a continuum from crisis intervention and intake procedures through hospital milieu treatment and out-patient care to discharge planning and rehabilitation efforts. Each technologist, of course, will not be equally prepared to discharge all of these functions, but rather his particular strengths will be influenced by the area of specialization in which he trains. The direct patient care offered by the technologist will be geared to such goals as growth, restoration, and maintenance, requiring therapeutic, rehabilitative, and supportive procedures as indicated.

Mental Health Technologists, as middle-level professionals, will be afforded job mobility with increasing responsibility. New and emerging mental health careers will be open to graduates who qualify as competent and sensitive mental health technologists, in a variety of mental health and related human service settings.

The existing manpower shortage in the mental health field has been amply documented over the past decade. The emergence of mental health centers to provide comprehensive coverage and continuity of care for all citizens has accentuated even further the manpower gap. This is a prevailing situation of national scope. Many varied mental health settings and related human service

*Source: College of Allied Health Professions, Hahnemann Medical College and Hospital 1976-1978 Catalog, Philadelphia.

agencies have shown an increasing interest in mental health services at the bachelor's level. Opportunities for employment exist in mental health centers, state hospitals, social service agencies, child-care services, as well as in the fields of rehabilitation and corrections. However, the program is not designed or intended to prepare students for entry into private practice. It is expected that graduates will seek employment in socially sanctioned service delivery systems where professional supervision will be available.

Program

The Mental Health Technology program at Hahnemann is unique in combining formal academic courses with supervised mental health training within the same organization structure. This combination, comprising the student's third and fourth years of college, leads to a Bachelor of Science degree. Initiated by the Hahnemann Department of Mental Health Sciences, the program provides the student with specialized training in the field of mental health. Approximately thirty students are accepted annually to begin the program each September.

The junior year is organized primarily around formal course work designed to impact a comprehensive understanding of human behavior in its environmental context. The approach is to view the individual as an integration of biological, psychological, social and cultural forces. During this period, the student is also familiarized with the structure and functions of mental health organizations with strong emphasis on service delivery in community mental health centers.

The senior year offers an eleven-month intensive training experience. The assignment area or service setting in which the student specializes is guided by the student's own interest and aptitude. Seminars are held concomitantly throughout most of the training phase with the aim of integrating theory and practice. The practicum may take place in either the Hahnemann Adult Psychiatric Service or the Children's Psychiatric Service. Institutions affiliated with Hahnemann may also be utilized for this purpose. Students receive their formal training in an in-patient or out-patient setting or in one of the services designed to meet the special needs of children or adults. This eleven-month practicum is designed to commence in mid-September at the inception of the

academic year. However, special arrangements can frequently be
made for individual students who wish to start during the preceding summer.

Each student is expected to demonstrate an inquiring mind
and to assume an active role in his or her own learning process.
The student is further expected to synthesize developing knowledge and skills in a pragmatic way that facilitates and promotes
the well-being of patient, family, and community.

Methods of evaluation will vary as they will be determined by
the individual instructor of each course. The most frequently
utilized procedures, however, will entail assigned papers, written
examinations and, occasionally, oral examinations. Class participation is encouraged and a student's contributions will often be
considered in the evaluation process.

Admission Requirements

All students seeking matriculation at the College must meet the
basic admission requirements described in a preceding section of
the catalog. Those applicants who appear qualified for admission
will be invited to participate in a personal interview conducted by
one or more members of the Department of Mental Health
Sciences.

Curriculum

All courses listed below are required for Mental Health Technology students. Additional students may be admitted to courses
by special arrangements with the program director.

Mental Health Technology Program

JUNIOR YEAR

M.H. 311	Behavioral Sciences I	2
M.H. 312	Behavioral Sciences II	2
M.H. 313	Behavioral Sciences III	2
M.H. 307	Cultural & Community I	2
M.H. 308	Cultural & Community II	2
M.H. 309	Cultural & Community III	2
M.H. 303	Personality & Psychotherapy I	2
M.H. 304	Personality & Psychotherapy II	2

M.H. 305	Personality & Psychotherapy III	2
M.H. 331	Orientation to Group Therapy	2
M.H. 332	Analysis of Group Development	2
M.H. 321	Community Mental Health	2
M.H. 325	Marriage & Family Dynamics	2
M.H. 342	Psychopathology I	2
M.H. 343	Psychopathology II	2
M.H. 336	Principles of Interviewing	2
M.H. 341	The Piagetian System	2
Math 343	Basic Statistics	3
Phys. 101	Anatomy & Physiology I	3
Phys. 102	Anatomy & Physiology II	3
	Total Quarter Hours for Junior Year	43

SENIOR YEAR

M.H. 351	Clinical Case Conference I	2
M.H. 352	Clinical Case Conference II	2
M.H. 353	Clinical Case Conference III	2
M.H. 373	The Chronic Schizophrenic Patient	2
M.H. 383	Mental Retardation	2
M.H. 361	Psychopharmacology	2
M.H. 372	Crisis Intervention	2
M.H. 382	Family Therapy	2
M.H. 381	Behavioral Disorders in Children & Adolescents	2
M.H. 371	Treatment Approaches to Low-Income Populations	2
M.H. 358	Mental Health Technology in Perspective	2
M.H. 391	Clinical Training I	7.5
(11 consecutive months: Mid-September Mid-August)		
M.H. 392	Clinical Training II	7.5
M.H. 393	Clinical Training III	7.5
M.H. 394	Clinical Training IV	7.5
	Total Quarter Hours for Senior Year	52
	Total Quarter Hours for Graduation	95

Appendix 5

COMPARISON OF THE MAJOR MENTAL HEALTH PROFESSIONS: PSYCHOLOGY, PSYCHIATRY, SOCIAL WORK*

By C. M. DeCato, Ph.D.

Profession	Training	Practice	Legal Ethical
Clinical Psychology	Four years liberal arts college leading to B.A. or B.S. Then some take two years graduate studies leading to M.A. or M.S. degree. Some go straight through graduate school to Ph.D. Depends on the particular graduate school. The graduate training usually includes supervised internship experience in a variety of work settings, such as mental hospitals and psychiatric clinics. Total time is from between four to eight years	Psychotherapies and psychological evaluations, consultation. The clinical psychologist may practice in psychiatric clinics, hospitals, community mental health centers, special schools for disturbed children, residential treatment centers for children. May establish a private independent practice. Often practice is combined with some teaching at graduate and undergraduate levels in college and universities.	Over forty states now license psychologists for independent practice. They are generally licensed to perform non-medical techniques such as psychotherapy and psychological evaluations. Each state has its own license, which must be studied to know specifically what the psychologist is allowed to do. Pennsylvania passed a licensing bill in the spring of 1972, which is effective as of November, 23, 1973. This bill specifies a Master's degree plus four years experience or

*DeCato, C.M.: Section of Psychology Education, Hahnemann Medical College and Hospital, Philadelphia, Pennsylvania, unpublished outline. Reprinted with permission of author.

Profession	Training	Practice	Legal Ethical
	on averages, bringing the total years of college level training to between eight and twelve years. The degree is the Doctor of Philosophy (PhD.). Some persons elect to take further supervised training in some specific area. This is called "Post-Doctoral" training. Usually extends for one or two years. Some new professional programs are forming in the U.S. which give intensive, highly, professional training. Some of these programs grant what is called a Doctor of Psychology degree (Psy.D.). Others still grant the Ph.D. degree. The Doctor of Psychology programs tends to be shorter as they omit the research training emphasized in most Ph.D. programs.	Clinical psychologists are also trained in the administration and interpretation of psychological scales sometimes called "tests." Testing has traditionally been part of their practice. May function as a consultant in mental health matters to agencies such as schools or industry. Some clinical psychologists devote a major portion of their time to private practice but the majority work for institutions at least part time.	a Ph.D plus two years experience to apply for the license. Boarding examinations are part of the license. Professional conduct is guided by a formal code of ethics established by the American Psychological Association (APA).
Psychiatry	Four years medical college leading to M.D. degree. States vary, some require one year internship. Then there are three years of residency training bringing total time of training to about eight years.	*Psychotherapy* (this does not differ from clinical psychologists). *Medical Treatments* of mentally ill (e.g., drugs, surgery, convulsive therapies). This does differ from psychologists who do not use medical procedures. In general psychiatry involves the	Licensed as an M.D.

Adult Basic Psychiatry:
Three years residency.
Adolescent Psychiatry:
Three years basic, one year of adolescent.
Child Psychiatry:
Two years basic, two years child.

Specific training programs vary. To know what a given program requires involves contacting persons in that program.

study, diagnosis and treatment of mental disorders.

May work in hospitals, psychiatric clinics, for children or adults, residential treatment programs, consultant to institutions and agencies on mental health matters and some teach in medical schools.

Social work

Four years of liberal arts college leading to a B.A. or B.S. degree.

Two years graduate studies and training leading to M.S.W. (Master of Social Work), or M.S.S. (Master of Social Services).

Some social workers elect special training in psychiatric settings which may equip them to engage in psychodiagnosis and psychotherapy. These persons are referred to as "Psychiatric Social Workers."

Wide range of employment situations: State and government agencies, psychiatric hospitals and clinics, child welfare agencies, community mental health, many types of institutions employ.

A relatively small number who have received training in psychotherapy may have private practices.

Generally not licensed. Following two years of supervised work in single setting receive A.C.S.W. certification (Academy of Certified Social Workers).

The Psychiatric Team: Traditionally, psychiatric clinics and hospitals have engaged psychologists, psychiatrists and social workers as teams with each discipline contributing to the examination, understanding, and treatment of the patient.

Appendix 6

WHO DOES WHAT
FOR VOLUNTEER SERVICES
CYCLE OF PROCESS*

	Volunteer-Coordinator or Director of Volunteers	*Agency Supervisor of Volunteer Service in Program*
WORK ANALYSIS	Establish Executive and staff support of need for Volunteer Services to carry out program goals and translate tasks into assignments for individual and group volunteers.	Find things volunteers could do to help, time and qualities required, job descriptions for entry jobs and promotion routes.
PROMOTION AND RECRUITMENT	Use all available media to describe opportunities to groups and individuals in community. Interview and refer volunteers appropriately.	In the community encourage volunteering for your agency and refer volunteers to coordinator for initial choices and recording of interests.
COUNSELING	Continuous process: matching volunteer interests and available time to needs, offering choices to volunteers.	See referred volunteers, test suitability to job requirements, assign to staff who will supervise them there or refer back to coordinator.
STANDARDS AND ORIENTATION	Describe background and program of agency, policies and standards to volunteers.	Introduce site ground rules, expectations about volunteers needs of people being served, schedule, duties.
TRAINING AND SUPERVISION	Plan with volunteers and staff continuing periodic events to train volunteers in groups. Use new films in field and round tables and volunteer feedback.	Give on the job supervision, involve volunteers in planning what they need to learn next, report staff and volunteer training needs to volunteer coordinator.
RECORDS AND REPORTS	Keep records of volunteer services by groups and individual volunteers; tailor information for Executive, and general public, volunteers as individuals.	Document services given, differences volunteers make, project future needs for volunteers for Coordinator.

*Source: Volunteer Action Council.